BLACK TORNADO

Also by Sandeep Unnithan

Operation X: The Untold Story of India's Covert Naval War in East Pakistan 1971

Praise for *Black Tornado: The Three Sieges of Mumbai 26/11*

'*Black Tornado's* biggest merit lies in its attention to detail; every counter-attack, hostage situation and bureaucratic decision is explained for the reader's benefit.' – *DNA*

'*Black Tornado* offers previously unshared details on the 26/11 terror attacks on Mumbai, and how, for the first time, all three armed forces systematically planned and thwarted the siege on the city in 2008.' – *Mid-day*

BLACK TORNADO

The Three Sieges of Mumbai 26/11

SANDEEP UNNITHAN

HarperCollins *Publishers* India

First published in India by
HarperCollins *Publishers* in 2014

HarperCollins Publishers India, Cyber City, Building 10-A, Gurugram,
Haryana-122002, India
www.harpercollins.co.in

2 4 6 8 10 9 7 5 3 1

This edition published in 2020 by HarperCollins India

P-ISBN: 978-93-5357-678-3
E-ISBN: 978-93-5357-679-0

Typeset in 12/18 Giovanni Book
Jojy Philip, New Delhi 110 015

Printed and bound at
MicroPrints India, New Delhi

MIX
Paper
FSC FSC™ C218906

This product is made of FSC®-certified and other controlled material.

HarperCollins Publishers, Macken House, 39/40 Mayor Street
Upper, Dublin 1, D01 C9W8, Ireland

Dedicated to the people of my city Mumbai
and all those working to make it safer

'Kal Roos ko bikharte dekha tha,
Ab India toot ta dekhenge,
Hum barq-e-jehad ke sholon mein,
America ko jalte dekhenge.'

(We saw Russia disintegrate,
Now we will see India fall apart,
In the flames of jehad,
We will see America ablaze)

'War cry of the Mujahideen'. Urdu slogan in the notebook of a Pakistani terrorist trainee in a terrorist training camp in Rishkhor, Afghanistan. December 2001.

Contents

Sequence of Events

59 Hours in Mumbai

Wednesday, 26 November 2008

16.00 MFV Kuber anchors off Mumbai. Waits for sunset.

20.30 Eight terrorists land at Machhimar Nagar by Zodiac. Split into five teams.

20.20 First team begins shooting spree at CST station.

21.38 Third team enters Taj Palace and starts shooting. Second team links up with Taj shooters.

21.40 Second team opens fire inside Leopold Café.

22.00 Fourth team abandons Zodiac, enters Trident-Oberoi hotel.

22.25 Fifth team enters Nariman House, shoots residents, takes hostages.

22.30 Maharashtra Chief Secretary asks Delhi to send NSG. Also asks Western Naval command, Mumbai, for marine commandos.

23.00 51 SAG sounds alert at Manesar complex, Haryana.

23.00 Navy harbour craft sets sail from naval dockyard Mumbai for MARCOS base, INS Abhimanyu.

23.20 Maharashtra Chief Secretary asks for army assistance.

Thursday, 27 November

00.00 Harbour craft reaches naval dockyard, Mumbai.

00.00 CST gunman Ajmal Kasab captured alive. Interrogated by Mumbai police at Nair hospital. Reveals plan, number of attackers.

00.18 NSG headquarters Delhi orders 51 SAG (CTTF-1) to move to Mumbai.
00.35 Army HQ Delhi orders five army columns, around 500 soldiers, to move to assist civil authority.
00.54 NSG leaves Manesar. Heads for ARC complex, Delhi airport.
01.40 51 SAG reaches ARC complex. Start loading up IL-76.
02.00 17 policemen killed, 35 injured in multiple attacks. Police withdraws from sieges.
02.00 Army sets up cordons around Leopold Café, Taj Palace and Tower, Oberoi Hotel, CST station, Cama Hospital.
02.00 One team of eight Marine Commandos arrives at Taj Palace.
02.00 Second team of MARCOS arrives at Trident-Oberoi. Attempts to go upstairs but beaten back by terrorists.
02.30 SAG's second unit, CTTF-2, with 148 commandos reaches Delhi airport.
03.00 IL-76 with NSG takes off from Delhi, heads to Mumbai.
05.00 IL-76 lands in Mumbai airport. Unloads aircraft, drives to South Mumbai.
05.00 16 more MARCOS arrives at Taj. Firefights with terrorists at The Chambers.
05.30 NSG brass briefed in Mumbai police control room.
06.00 Terrorists retreat after firefight with MARCOS. The Chambers' guests evacuated.
07.30 NSG HQ Delhi asks CTTF-2 to leave for Mumbai. They board ARC IL-76 that returns from Mumbai.
09.00 51 SAG arrives at the Oberoi.
09.30 SAG takes over Taj hotels. Split forces to comb Palace & Tower.
09.30 Detailed interrogation of CST gunman Ajmal Kasab captured alive by police.
10.00 IL-76 with SAG's CTTF-2 takes off from Delhi airport.
11.00 SAG teams walk up the Oberoi for room clearance operations.
12.00 CTTF-2 lands at Mumbai airport. Drives to South Mumbai. Force split between Taj and Nariman House sieges.
15.00 Mumbai police brief CTTF-2 on situation in Nariman House. SAG begins recce of building.
17.30 SAG makes contact with terrorists in Room 1856 of the Oberoi.
18.30 SAG lays sniper cordon around Nariman House.
20.00 One terrorist killed in firefight at the Oberoi.
21.30 Electricity to Nariman House cut off. SAG's first attempt to enter building from ground beaten back by terrorists.

Friday, 28 November

00.30	Second terrorist killed by NSG at the Oberoi.
01.00	SAG evacuates civilians from buildings adjacent to Nariman House.
01.00	Major Sandeep Unnikrishnan killed in firefight with terrorists.
03.00	SAG clears all 21 floors of Taj Tower. Location handed over to police.
07.00	IAF Mi-17 drops SAG commandos on roof of Nariman House.
07.00	Body of second terrorist found at the Oberoi. All hotel guests evacuated.
07.00	All hotel guests evacuated from Taj Tower by police.
07.55	SAG commando Gajender Singh killed during room clearance operation on fourth floor of Nariman House.
09.30	Major Unnikrishnan's body recovered. Pause in Taj operations.
16.00	SAG reaches north wing of Taj Palace. Firefight with terrorists.
17.00	SAG storm fourth floor of Nariman House. Kill both terrorists.
18.30	SAG clears the Oberoi. Hands over to police

Saturday, 29 November 2008

02.00	Firefight rages at Harbor Bar, Wasabi restaurants of Taj Palace.
06.00	Fire breaks out in restaurants and bar. Three of the four terrorists shot down as they flee. Body of fourth found inside.
07.00	Fire in north wing of Taj Palace doused.

Preface

Six years ago, ten heavily armed terrorists from the Lashkar-e-Taiba (LeT) nearly set India and Pakistan on the brink of war. Using a stealthy, seaborne insertion tactic pioneered by Palestinian terrorists decades ago, the military-style assault on Mumbai achieved its initial objective: complete surprise. It was the world's first hybrid terrorist attack – a deadly witches' brew of car bombs and well-trained gunmen swarming across multiple locations to achieve what the military calls the penetration of an adversary's OODA cycle: a sequence of Observe, Orient, Decide and Act.

The two landing sites and the targets – two iconic five star hotels, a Jewish centre and a prominent railway station complex – had been meticulously recced by an LeT ferret planted in Mumbai. These facts are so well known that they barely need repetition.

The attacks possibly had dual tactical objectives. To extract a video-game-counter like toll of civilian lives and later, to lay prolonged, multiple sieges in

India's commercial capital. The strategic objectives also appeared to be two-fold. To strike at the booming Indian economy and heighten border tensions which could jeopardize Pakistan President Asif Ali Zardari's peace outreach towards India.

The feeble reception that awaited the gunmen in Mumbai was inexplicable. For at least two years prior to the attacks, Indian intelligence agencies issued at least twenty-six alerts warning of possible Fedayeen strikes, seaborne attacks and multi-target raids. Yet this spreading bloom of alerts, did not cause even a murmur and were instead, lazily passed down from the Central intelligence agencies down the bureaucratic chain in the Mumbai police. Hotels on the target list did not even install basic measures like doorframe metal detectors or blast protected doors or even rehearse emergencies.

The Mumbai city police, steeped in its mythology of gangland wars, fumbled at first to identify the unfolding threat. When they had established it to be an overwhelming terror attack, they unaccountably withdrew from all the locations. They lacked the capability to respond.

When the armed forces were called in, it resulted in India's first counter-terrorist operation involving all three armed forces – the first responders, the naval commandos, infantry units of the army that laid cordons around the locations and the air force pilots who flew in the NSG.

This book is named after the operation launched by the National Security Guard, specifically its 51 Special Action Group, to rescue the civilians who were trapped in the three sieges and to neutralize eight terrorists. There has been no detailed analysis or account of this joint but loosely coordinated military action. This book attempts to put the military aspect of this response into perspective through interviews with the marine commandos, personnel from the infantry unit based in the city and the NSG's strike element, the 51 Special Action Group. The narrative is focused on the SAG that handled, in public glare, forty-eight of the sixty hours of the operations.

The Black Cats were to be a repository of specialized counter-terrorist knowledge. Like its symbol, Lord Vishnu's 108-edged discus, the Sudarshan Chakra, they were to fly out, dispatch evil and return to base. The discus had, however, turned into a slow bludgeon as early as 2002. SAG commandos took five hours to reach Gandhinagar, the capital of Gujarat on 24 September 2002 after two LeT terrorists massacred 33 visitors to the Swaminarayan temple. Inadequate personal protection gear led to the deaths of two commandos as they moved against the two terrorists later that evening.

As we shall see, various events and processes blunted their edge.

A Wednesday

At 11.30 p.m. on Wednesday, 4 March 1975, eight Palestinian terrorists in two inflatable rubber crafts with outboard motors landed on a beach in Tel Aviv. They had set sail from their base in southern Lebanon and intended to capture either the Manshia Youth Club or the Tel Aviv Opera House. They had, however, lost their way. They walked into the four-storey Savoy Hotel located 100 metres away from Jerusalem beach. It was the only building on the street that was brightly lit. The terrorists took ten hostages. They wanted Israel to release twenty Palestinian terrorists held captive by the Israelis, and an aircraft to fly them to Damascus. At 4.20 a.m. next day, Israeli forces stormed the hotel. The terrorists were barricaded on the top floor with all the hostages. In the ensuing firefight, eight hostages lost their lives. Three Israeli soldiers, including the commanding officer Uzi Yairi, were killed. Seven of the terrorists blew themselves up, destroying the top floor of the building. Only one was captured alive.

Target Mumbai

Mumbai, India's commercial capital, was one of the most frequently bombed cities in the world in 2008. Between March 1993 and July 2006, the city witnessed a dozen bomb attacks of varying intensity which used improvised explosive devices (IEDs), some fashioned out of sophisticated plastic explosives with timer switches, others pressure cookers modified with locally procured ammonium nitrate. These bomb attacks had killed 516 citizens and injured 1,952. Unlike Kabul and Baghdad, the state was not in the grip of civil war. It was, however, on the front lines of a new and dangerous kind of terrorism: a proxy war against India's hinterland that had spilled out of Jammu and Kashmir.

The twelve sequential bomb attacks of 12 March1993 accounted for the city's largest body count: 257. The plastic explosives were packed in vehicles parked near the Bombay Stock Exchange; the Air India building; inside a double-decker city bus that passed near the regional passport office; at a petrol pump near the Shiv Sena Bhavan, the cream-coloured, four-storey headquarters of the right-wing political party, at three five-star hotels; a cinema in central Mumbai; and at the Zaveri Bazaar in central Mumbai. Hand grenades were flung at the tarmac of the Sahar International Airport and the fishermen's colony in Mahim, suburban Mumbai. Jeeps, cars and scooters were turned into bombs using a shipment of nearly 1.5 tonnes of RDX. The deadly plastic explosive came from Karachi. It was landed using boats on a deserted coastline on the mainland south-east of Mumbai. The shipment, still in cardboard cartons with the marking 'Wah Nobel (Pvt) Ltd. Wah Cant', was traced to the state-owned public limited company located in the Wah cantonment, 30 km north-west of Rawalpindi, Pakistan. It was clear that the serial bomb plot had not only the blessings but the active collaboration of Pakistan's state actors, particularly the army and its Inter-Services Intelligence (ISI).

The blasts came less than two months after the Hindu–Muslim communal riots in January 1993 that lasted twenty-two days and resulted in 900 killings. The rioting was triggered by the demolition of the Babri Masjid by Hindu fanatics in the state of Uttar Pradesh on 6 December 1992. The 12 March blasts were purported to be revenge attacks by the city's Muslim-dominated underworld, dominated by the Dubai-based Dawood Ibrahim, a fugitive from India since 1983. The offshore don tapped into the hurt caused within his community by the savage riots following the demolition of the Babri Masjid, and used his old gold smuggling routes and underworld network to bring explosives into the city.

There were ten other bomb attacks of varying intensity between 1993 and 2003. On 25 August 2003, fifty-two persons died in twin blasts at the Gateway of India and at the Zaveri Bazaar, a crowded market in central Mumbai. It was the largest attack since 1993. Three years later, the horror returned. In July 2006, 200 persons were killed in seven blasts inside the city's lifeline, its commuter trains. Yet, these attacks had failed to shatter the city's standing as India's financial hub or deter its citizenry. The attacks were anonymous and faceless. The city had never known the terror of gun-wielding assailants.

But it almost did. The March 1993 serial blasts were only Phase 1, and Phase 2 was just as deadly. Over 400 Chinese Type 56 assault rifles and Arges hand grenades were brought in with the RDX shipment from Pakistan. Some of these rifles and grenades would also be wielded by nineteen Muslim youth, members of the Ibrahim crime syndicate, who had specifically been trained by the ISI in Pakistan. The nineteen youth worked for Ibrahim Mushtaq Abdul Razak 'Tiger' Memon, a Dawood Ibrahim lieutenant. Tiger Memon instructed them to storm the Mantralaya, headquarters of the state administration in south Mumbai; the Brihanmumbai Municipal Corporation (BMC) building near the

Chhatrapati Shivaji Terminus (CST) station; and the Shiv Sena headquarters. They were to inflict maximum casualties using the Type 56 rifles and hand grenades.

Phase 2 was never implemented. In the melee that followed the blasts, these youth panicked. Their leaders, Bashir Khan and Anwar Theba, fled. They abandoned their cache – assault rifles, pistols, ammunition and hand grenades near Mumbai's famous Siddhivinayak temple at Worli. Possibly it was because they were leaderless: the main conspirator, Tiger Memon, had fled to Dubai just hours before the serial blasts. His extended family, including parents and four brothers, their wives and children had reached Dubai four days earlier. Perhaps the would-be attackers lacked the motivation, training and indoctrination to mow down their fellow citizens. Walking away from car bombs was easier.

Indian investigators quickly forgot about this plot that was not executed. They focused on framing charges against the serial blast conspirators. Part of this arms cache was to have been handed out to members of the city's Muslim community as protection. The plotters feared Hindu mobs would seek revenge for the blasts. At least one Type 56 rifle found its way into the hands of popular movie star Sanjay Dutt. He had it home-delivered by his movie producer friends and Dawood Ibrahim acolytes, Hanif Kadawala and Samir Hingora. This relationship detailed the proximity of a certain section of the film fraternity with the underworld both before and after the 1993 blasts. In fact, in the 1990s, the movie industry was caught in the crossfire of gang wars as splinter groups of the Dawood Ibrahim syndicate – Chhota Rajan and Abu Salem – extorted protection money from the film industry and construction business. On 12 September 1992, twenty-four members of the Dawood syndicate stormed the JJ hospital where Shailesh Haldankar, a gangster from the rival Arun Gawli faction was admitted. Haldankar had gunned down Dawood's hotelier brother-in-law Ibrahim Parkar. The gangsters reportedly fired over 100 rounds, killing Haldankar and two police constables who were guarding him. Among the firearms they used was an AK-47, the first time the assault rifle had been used by the underworld.

The Mumbai police was by the mid-1990s solely focused on the underworld. Specially set up encounter squads wiped out underworld shooters in extrajudicial killings. Its sole encounter with AK-47-wielding terrorist Sikh militants holed up outside Mumbai in 1992 was quickly forgotten. The police force strangely lacked any offensive capability against terrorists. Frequent attempts to raise Special Weapons and Tactics (SWAT) police units, modelled on the New Delhi–based National Security Guard (NSG), failed to take off.

The first attempt was in 1993, soon after the serial blasts. Col Mahendra Pratap Chaudhary, a retired commando instructor, trained a group of 400 motorcycle-borne policemen. He chose to make Mumbai his post-retirement home and offered his services to the city police. The offer was taken up by then police commissioner Mahesh Narain Singh. The police commandos were equipped with 9 mm pistols, carbines and AK-47s, and split into buddy pairs that would use motorcycles to negotiate Mumbai's log-jammed traffic to swiftly reach an emergency. The force did not see action. After Singh's tenure ended in 1995, the unit rapidly wilted into disuse and was finally disbanded.

In 2003, the Mumbai police created quick-response teams (QRTs) comprising eight officers and forty-eight men. These policemen were put through an eighteen-month course by the State Reserve Police Force (SRPF) in Pune, followed by a three-month course by the NSG at Manesar near Delhi. But the QRTs had not fired a shot since September 2007: they had run out of ammunition to practise with.

The city police was worse off. Overworked, under-equipped and short-staffed as they were, training received short shrift. The police were armed with the .303 Lee Enfield rifle and its single-shot Indian improvisation, the .410 musket. The iconic .303 had first seen action in the second Boer War in 1899. In the hands of well-drilled infantrymen, the bolt-action rifle could be devastating in long-range engagements on the plains. It was useless for urban close-quarter battles in the hands of untrained police constables. The unavailability of training ammunition only made matters worse. The state police needed ammunition worth Rs 65 crore if each policeman had to fire the mandatory forty rounds each. They, however, got only Rs 3 crore to buy ammunition for the financial year 2008–09. The police had asked for 1.6 lakh rounds of AK-47 ammunition for its AK-47 assault rifle arsenal, but hadn't received even the 38,195 rounds that were finally sanctioned. Most AK-47 ammunition was diverted to the police forces in the state's eastern districts battling left-wing extremism.

Mumbai seemed uneasily insulated against a peculiar and deadly Metropolitan terror which had intensified by 2008. In May that year, nine serial blasts in marketplaces in Jaipur killed sixty-three persons. Eight low-intensity blasts in Bangalore in July killed two persons and seventeen serial blasts in Ahmedabad the same month killed twenty-nine persons. Twenty-one persons were killed in five serial blasts in Delhi's busy markets on 13 September. Each attack was immediately preceded by a triumphant email from the Indian Mujahideen, ostensibly a home-grown terrorist outfit, claiming credit for the attacks. The bomb attacks came at a time when India was riding the global economic crest with a growth rate of over 8 per cent, second only to China. A January 2007 projection by investment bank Goldman Sachs predicted that India could overtake Britain to be the fifth largest economy in a decade and the second largest by 2050. A robust domestic market shielded the country from the global financial meltdown which began in 2007. Yet, it seemed, there was no escaping the bombs placed in cycles and motorbikes parked in marketplaces to randomly target Indian civilians. The larger motive, however, was clear. The blasts targeted India's growth engines, its cities.

Prime Minister Manmohan Singh, one of the architects of the 1991 reforms that triggered off India's economic boom, pointed an accusatory finger across the border. 'Pakistan-based terrorist outfits are constantly trying to set up new modules within the country,' he said, addressing a conference of state governors in New Delhi on 18 September 2008. The blasts were 'a matter of utmost concern', he said, admitting that the attacks had revealed vast gaps in intelligence.

Intelligence wings of the state police were the weakest link in an information-gathering chain, critical to tracking and detecting terror modules sprouting across India. The political leadership saw these departments as dumping grounds for unpopular police officials or simply as tools for gathering information on political adversaries. Most states lacked a separate cadre and staffed their wings by personnel deputed from the regular force. The wings depended on handouts from the Central agencies, the

Research and Analysis Wing (R&AW) and the Intelligence Bureau (IB) which they sometimes dismissed as 'routine weather forecasts' because they were not actionable.

Beginning in 2006, R&AW and IB had begun alerting the Mumbai police of the LeT's preparations to infiltrate fidayeen suicide terrorists into the city through the sea. By 2008, these alerts had built up into an ominous crescendo. The Ram Pradhan committee that probed the Mumbai police's response to the attack mentioned a total of twenty-six intelligence alerts which warned of major terrorist attacks. The agencies detailed an astonishingly long list of hotels and government buildings as targets. Three alerts even mentioned specific dates for terrorist attacks on Mumbai: 20 August 2006, 24 May and 11 August 2008. Six alerts spoke of the possibility of a seaborne attack. Eleven spoke of the possibility of simultaneous attacks and three alerts even mentioned fidayeen attacks.

The sheer build-up of these warnings should have triggered off an alarm in the upper echelons of the police force and led to a detailed threat perception study. The alerts were, instead, mechanically handed down its bureaucracy to the 'zone' as they called a precinct with four police stations.

On 26 June, the additional commissioner of the Anti-Terrorism Squad (ATS) informed Vishwas Nangre-Patil, the deputy commissioner of police in charge of the

Mumbai police's Zone 1, that two terrorists might have entered India in May 2008 and may well be in Mumbai. Only one of the targets the alert mentioned – a temple near Shivaji Park in Dadar – fell outside Nangre-Patil's precinct which extended from Marine Drive to Colaba. The targets included a site code-named Leopold, the Bombay High Court, the director general of police's office located near the Taj Mahal Palace and Tower and the offices of the Department of Atomic Energy building next to it. Nangre-Patil immediately alerted Deepak Vishwasrao, the senior police inspector in charge of the Colaba Police Station. The police determined one of the targets to be the popular tourist bar, the Leopold Café on Colaba Causeway whose owners they alerted. On 11 August, Nangre-Patil and the municipal authorities began a drive to clear hawkers from the pavement in front of the café.

The alerts from the Central agencies continued to come in and the Ram Pradhan Committee meticulously recounted the sequence of events and police responses. On 24 September, the IB informed the Maharashtra director general of police Anami Roy that the Lashkar-e-Taiba (LeT) had been showing 'interest' in launching attacks on Mumbai. The list of possible targets included the Taj Mahal Palace and Tower, the Sardar Vallabhai Patel Stadium, the Sea Rock Hotel and the Taj Land's End the last two located in Bandra, the JW Marriot Hotel in Juhu and the Juhu Aerodrome in suburban Mumbai. This alert was passed on to the police commissioner the following day. Four days later, Nangre-Patil and Senior PI Vishwasrao visited the Taj. The officers met the hotel general manager Karambir Kang, the security manager Sunil Kudiyadi and Mahavir Singh Rathod, security head of all Taj hotels. They discussed the various threat scenarios – a suicide attack, planting of VBIEDs and explosives.

The policemen had come with a list of suggestions to beef up security. They wanted the CCTV systems of both Taj buildings to be integrated and manned continuously. Only one gate of the hotel should be kept open with door frame metal detectors, they advised. On 30 September, the two police officers were back at the hotel. This time, they briefed hotel authorities on the model security instructions issued for the Bombay Stock Exchange building where eighty-four persons had died in the March 1993 attacks. On 2 October, Nangre-Patil detailed twenty-six steps to augment the Taj's security. In a letter to Senior PI Deepak Vishwasrao, Nangre-Patil suggested positioning snipers on the terrace of the Taj, police guards at the entrance, integrating the CCTVs of both wings and manning them round the clock and installing door frame metal detectors to check visitors at the entrance. Nangre-Patil also suggested closing the hotel's Northcote gate, an open entrance at the southern end of the old wing named for a nursing home that stood across the road. This unguarded entrance led visitors into the heart of the hotel. On 16 October, the senior police inspector wrote to Nangre-Patil to report that the hotel management had been instructed on the points raised by the DCP. If there was any urgency in the police, it did not show on the ground. On 13 October, the Mumbai police withdrew the two policemen it had posted outside the Taj hotel. The hotels did not demand additional police cover. It was business as usual in Mumbai.

On 30 October, the combined operations room in the coastal town of Vadinar, Gujarat, flashed an alert to the Central intelligence agencies in Delhi. The alert was extremely unusual because the Ops Room, a grouping of navy, coast guard, Intelligence Bureau, Border Security Force and army representatives, rarely issued such warnings. The alert said that thirty terrorists were crossing over for an attack within the next thirty days. Mumbai was not mentioned, but the missive did not trigger any alarm. It was buried within Delhi's bureaucratic intelligence maze.

Meanwhile, somewhere in Pakistan, the forgotten Phase 2 of the 1993 blasts was being put into action.

Mumbai Under Attack

Bharat Tandel sat at his favourite post-dinner spot in Colaba, the Machhimar Nagar boat ramp. The twenty-foot-wide ramp, where fishermen launched their boats into the sea, was one of the few open spaces in the densely packed fishing colony in south Mumbai. The cool sea breeze whipped around Tandel's gnarled, weather-beaten face as he stared out at the fishing boats that bobbed at anchor in the Backbay Reclamation, an unfinished real estate project that was now a fishing harbour. Tandel looked around, trying to spot his own boat in the high tide. On nights like this, there were usually dozens of fisherfolk like him around. But tonight they were all in their homes watching Suresh Raina and Rohit Sharma hammer the English bowling attack in the fifth One-Day International cricket match in Cuttack's Barabati stadium. The fifty-one-year-old fisherman didn't care. He hated cricket.

So it was that he saw something unusual. A dirty black-and-yellow Zodiac inflatable rubber boat headed for

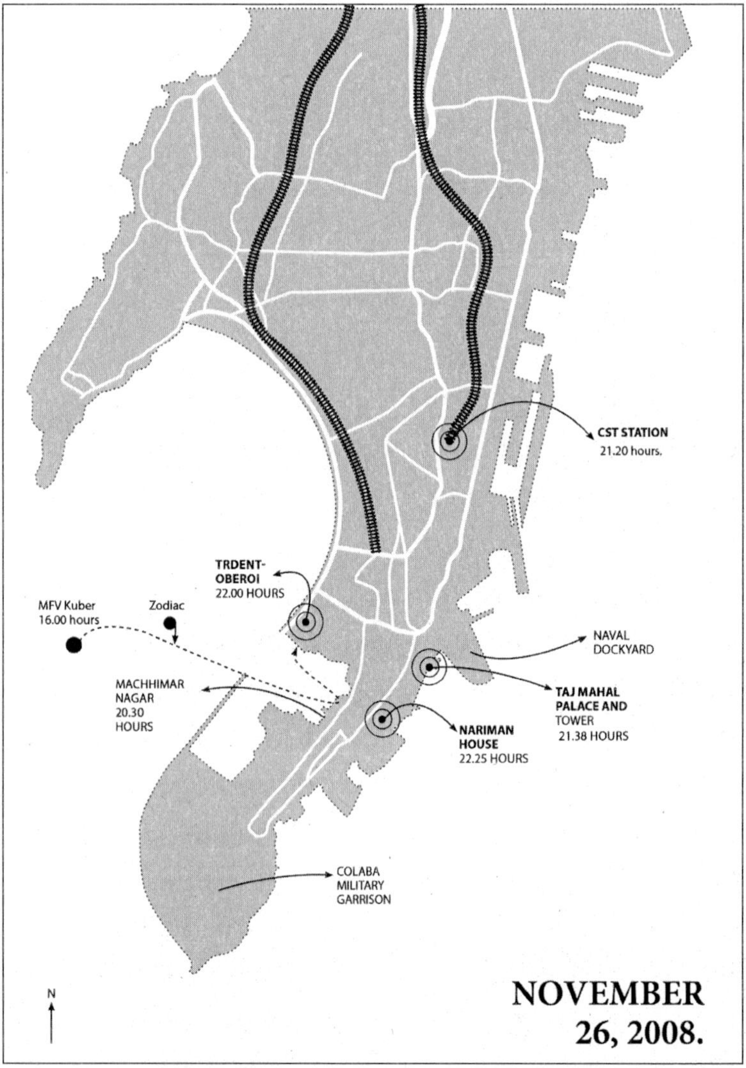

the ramp across the boats lined up there, towards him. The growl of the boat engine ceased and gave way to the sploshing of oars. Two of the men were furiously rowing towards the shore. At the ramp, one of the crew stepped out and held the boat with a rope and seven young men sprang out of the boat. Fair, clean-shaven and in their twenties, they didn't appear to be locals. They wore orange life jackets over their clothes and were in their underpants. 'Must be those rich kids from the H2O,' Tandel thought. H2O was a water-sports complex on the iconic Chowpatty beach further north. Speedboats from there occasionally ventured here.

The boys tossed their life jackets back into the dinghy, put their trousers on and flung haversacks over their backs. Tandel saw his neighbour Bharat Tamore, a steward at the Taj who had stopped by on his way to a late shift at the hotel, challenge the youth. One of them shot back at him, '*Hum pehle se hi tang hain. Hume pareshaan mat karo.*' (We are already quite stressed. Don't pester us.)

'*Kya hai ...?*' Tandel asked them in an avuncular tone as they passed by. 'Tension *mein hai*,' one of them snarled and walked past him. The two men who had stayed back in the Zodiac yanked the starter cord and gunned the Yamaha outboard motor. The dinghy turned around and raced away into the darkness with a throaty roar. Tandel soon forgot the five-minute incident and went back to staring at the sea.

The eight young men lugged their heavy backpacks and briskly walked onto Prakash Pethe Marg, just 50 metres past the ramp. Here they said their goodbyes and split into pre-decided buddy pairs. It was the culmination of a long journey that had begun four days earlier.

These ten men – soon to be the familiar faces in India as the Mumbai terror attackers – set sail from Karachi on 22 November on board a small cargo vessel, the *Al-Husseini* owned by the Lashkar-e-Taiba military commander Zakiur Rahman Lakhvi.

The Lashkar-e-Taiba or the army of the pure was a Pakistani militant group with roots in the covert war to expel the Soviets from Afghanistan. Founded by a radical Ahle-Hadith preacher Hafiz Mohammed Saeed in 1990, it was a Janus-faced organization. Its charitable arm, the Jamaat-ud-Dawa, ran schools and hospitals across Pakistan. Its military arm, the LeT, recruited and trained Pakistani civilians, mostly from its largest province, Punjab, through three-month-long guerrilla courses in paramilitary camps. They were then infiltrated across a heavily militarized and disputed 740-km Line of Control (LOC) to fight Indian security forces in Jammu and Kashmir. Unlike other militant groups, the LeT was distinctly proximate to the Pakistan army. Every LeT leader was 'handled' by a serving officer from the Pakistan army's Directorate for Inter-Services Intelligence or ISI. So enmeshed was the LeT with the state, and so vital were they to calibrate its secret war in Kashmir, that they were often called 'sarkari mujahid' (government holy warriors) inside Pakistan.

The ten terrorists were 'fidayeens' or suicide commandos, the deadliest weapon in the LeT arsenal. They were launched for attacks against high-profile targets in Jammu and Kashmir and elsewhere in the Indian hinterland. These attacks began in 1999 and had peaked by 2001, which saw twenty-nine fidayeen strikes that killed 161 security personnel.

The attackers were all between the ages of eighteen and twenty-five, hand-picked by expert trainers who looked for a mixture of exceptional fitness, high motivation that would allow them to fight to the end, qualities found only in roughly one among nearly 200 recruits. They were then coached, indoctrinated and launched for the only mission of their lives.

The start of their journey had been carefully selected. On 17 November, the northern Arabian Sea resounded with the high-pitched whine of gas turbines, the drone of maritime patrol aircraft and the chatter of high-frequency communication as warships, patrol aircraft and helicopters of the Indian Navy's sword arm, the Western Fleet, manoeuvred in the 'Defence of Gujarat' exercise. DGX, for short, practised much more than just the defence of India's westernmost state against a seaborne attack during war. It was designed to secure India's energy corridor to West Asia from where over 60 per cent of oil supplies flowed. Then, on 22 November, as DGX came to a close, the radio chatter dropped to normal. The warships headed back to their home port in Mumbai. The coast, quite literally, was clear.

But the *Al-Husseini* could not enter Indian waters without being spotted by the Indian Navy or the Indian Coast Guard. At around 3 p.m. on 23 November, the LeT vessel lured and captured an Indian fishing trawler, the MFB *Kuber*. The *Kuber*'s four-member crew were taken prisoner on board the *Al-Husseini* and later murdered. The captain of the Indian trawler, Amar Singh Solanki, was asked to take the ten gunmen and their deadly cargo towards Mumbai. At gunpoint, Solanki steered the deadly Trojan horse nearly 500 nautical miles south, through the patrol areas of the Indian Navy and the Coast Guard in the north Arabian Sea, never straying more than 80 km away from the coastline. He brought the *Kuber* to a spot nearly 4 nautical miles west of Mumbai, a spot the gunmen located on their hand-held Global Positioning System (GPS). The trawler waited here for three hours, the horizon crowned by the city skyline. As the sun set over the city, the ten-man team contacted their handlers in Pakistan. They were instructed to kill their hapless captive, sink the trawler and sail on board the rubber dinghy into Mumbai. They complied, but only partially. As Solanki lay with his throat slit in the engine room, the gunmen inflated the rubber dinghy and lowered it into the sea. They briefly panicked when they mistook an approaching boat for a naval vessel, hastily clambering into their eleven-seater craft and headed for the shore. In the melee, they failed to pull out the seacocks that would sink the trawler as instructed. They left behind a drifting *Kuber* and a Thuraya satellite phone onboard.

Once on the city road, six of them flagged down the final transport to their destinations: two black-and-yellow taxicabs. One cab took four team members to the Taj hotel. The other one took the rest. Abu Soheb and Nazir alighted near Colaba Causeway, and the other two, Ismail Khan and Ajmal Kasab, went on up to CST. Abu Umar and Babar Imran crossed the road and spotted the gap in a wall where a narrow pedestrian path led into Colaba Causeway.

The team members hefted a three-foot-long haversack that weighed at least 15 kg. In it was an AK-47 assault rifle with a side-folding metal butt and six magazines each with thirty rounds. Each bag also had over 200 rounds of 7.62×39 mm loose ammunition, a dozen hand grenades, a 'Star' pistol and three spare magazines in a waist pouch. Each person also carried an 8-kg IED that had a programmable electronic timer switch and contained nearly 5 kg of RDX and 3 kg of tightly packed shrapnel. The team also carried a mobile phone with an Indian SIM card. A GPS handset with pre-fed coordinates on maps allowed each of the buddy pairs to precisely navigate to their targets. They had come prepared for war. Perhaps the most deceptive element in Mission Mumbai's exhaustive planning was the poisonous sting in the tail. When the horror was over its dead perpetrators would leave behind enough false trails to implicate Indians for the Pakistani deep state's most spectacular covert thrust. Each attacker wore a red thread or 'kalava' around his wrist, bought by LeT mole for Rs 20 each from near the Siddhivinayak temple. The SIM cards in their Nokia 1200 series mobile phones, which they would use to speak with their handlers in Pakistan, were bought in India. They also carried fake student identity cards from the Arunodaya Degree College in Hyderabad. Ajmal Kasab was 'Sameer Choudhary'. Ismail Khan was 'Naraish Verma'.

21.20 Hours / CST Station

The taxi Mohammed Ajmal Amir Kasab and Ismail Khan had hailed pulled inside the Chhatrapati Shivaji Terminus (as the magnificent 120-year-old Victorian Gothic structure was now called). They had left behind an IED, set to explode an hour later, under the driver's seat. They walked among the thousands of passengers waiting to board trains in one of India's busiest stations. Over 3.5 million people passed under its arches each day.

The duo then entered the large public lavatory, zipped open their haversacks and clipped a double magazine onto their rifles. The magazines were bound with duct tape, to allow for rapid reloads. They slung their rucksacks on one shoulder, leaving their firing arm free, a shooting technique taught to US Navy Seals. They emerged onto the concourse with their Kalashnikovs cocked, and opened fire. They had turned into what an October 2008 US Department of Homeland Security brochure called 'active shooters', 'individuals actively engaged in killing or attempting to kill people in a confined and populated area with no pattern or method to their selection of victims'.

Kasab and Ismail shot from the hip, in precise controlled bursts. Their walk was confident and unhurried. Their targets were the thousands of railway passengers – men, women and children – who waited on the concourse for the early long-distance trains that would take them to their native towns in UP and Bihar. CCTV footage on the concourse showed most of the policemen, armed with bamboo canes, fleeing like Keystone Kops. One constable attempted to fire back, but his poorly maintained .303 rifle jammed. In desperation, his comrade flung a plastic chair at the terrorists. Inspector Shashank Shinde, the railway police station-in-charge, rallied around a small team of policemen on the platform to lead a fightback. But his heroic effort was in vain. Kasab and Khan mowed down Shinde and three constables. They were done in by poor weaponry and lack of training – the bolt-action rifles they carried were designed at roughly the same time as the colonial-era station. Most policemen hadn't fired a shot in years. By the time the well-armed duo stopped shooting, fifty-eight persons lay dead and 104 injured. When social worker Santosh Koutlkar, twenty-six, entered the concourse shortly after the terrorists had walked away, it was quiet as a grave. There was no hum of passengers, no din of train announcements from the public address system. The stillness was interrupted by weak voices of *bachao, bachao* from survivors among the knots of bloody and mangled bodies.

Ismail Khan and Kasab were to have climbed into the CST building with hostages and hold out for a long siege. The resistance from the police, however feeble, diverted them from their main target. They headed up a flight of stairs at the centre of the station's suburban platforms but it was a foot overbridge that led outside the station complex. The active shooters were on the loose in Mumbai.

They walked into a lane leading to the six-storey government-run Cama and Albless Hospital for women and children which they mistook for a residential building. They scaled a rear gate and shot dead two unarmed security guards, Baban Ughade and Bhanu Narkar, who tried to shut the gates. Hospital staff had been alerted by the melee at the nearby CST station. Now, as they saw the gunmen entering their building, nurses and staff switched off lights and locked down the wards to protect over 200 frightened patients, most of them expectant mothers. The duo stalked the darkened corridors, looking for hostages. The hospital staff's ploy worked. As the terrorists exited the hospital after a futile search, they were challenged by a seven-man police team led by Additional Commissioner of Police Sadanand Date. In the exchange of fire, the duo killed Sub-inspector Prakash More and Constable Vijay Khandekar. Date was hit by grenade splinters, his 9 mm pistol jammed as he attempted to fire. The duo continued walking down the narrow Rang Bhavan Lane between St Xavier's College and Cama Hospital. They were frantically hunting for a getaway vehicle when they saw the incoming lights of a white Toyota Qualis minivan. It carried seven policemen, including the Maharashtra Anti-Terrorist Squad (ATS) chief Hemant Karkare, his deputy, Additional Commissioner Ashok Kamte, and Senior Police Inspector Vijay Salaskar. Kasab and Khan took cover on either side of a narrow lane and ambushed the minivan, raking it with AK-47 fire. As the bullet-ridden vehicle ground to a halt, they walked towards it and pulled out the bodies of the three senior officers. Kasab took an AK-47 and two magazines from Ashok Kamte's body. The bodies of Sub-inspector Bapusaheb Durgude and constables Jaywant Patil and Yogesh Patil lay in the rear. An injured head constable, Arun Jadhav, played dead. The duo then commandeered the Qualis and drove out to continue their mayhem on the city streets.

The two of them shot from inside the moving vehicle at a small group of waiting journalists and policemen at the junction of the landmark Metro cinema just 300 metres away from the hospital. They drove the police vehicle 2 km south, to Nariman Point, the city's business district, and abandoned it at a stone's throw from the Vidhan Bhavan building and the Oberoi Hotel. Here, Kasab and Khan commandeered a Skoda Laura from three terrified civilians and sped along the Queen's Necklace, towards the Girgaum Chowpatty sea-front, Mumbai's most famous public beach,3 km north. They came up against a police barricade at Girgaum Chowpatty. It was here that their unfamiliarity with the Skoda's unique reverse gear ended the chase. The gear stick has to be depressed before being shifted forward. Ismail Khan's frantic attempts to reverse only resulted in the car repeatedly surging into the road divider. The police at the barricade closed in. Ismail Khan pulled his pistol out and shot at the policemen, who fired back and killed him. Assistant Sub-inspector Tukaram Ombale meanwhile grappled with Kasab who had emerged from the passenger seat. In the process, Ombale took a full burst of bullets from Kasab's AK-47 on his chest. Kasab was overpowered and beaten by the policemen till he lost consciousness. He was taken under escort to the Nair Hospital in central Mumbai and attended to, just as the hundreds of other Mumbaikars wounded in the strikes. 'Please sir,' he pleaded with one of the policemen guarding him, 'I have done what I came to do. Please kill me.'

21.40 Hours / Leopold Café

The hawkers on the pavement of Colaba Causeway thought Abu Soheb and Abu Umar were tourists. The kind 'drawn like moths to a Kingfisher flame', as *Lonely Planet* puts it while writing about Leopold Café. The duo had got off the taxi and crossed the road to stand outside the landmark watering hole. They chatted on their mobile phones, then turned, bent down, unzipped their haversacks, inserted the twin magazines into their AK-47s, cocked their weapons and entered Leopold. They fired blindly all across the bar, killing ten diners, and flung a grenade that exploded near the cash counter at the far end. Soheb and Umar deftly changed magazines and sprayed a few more rounds inside to ensure there were no survivors. The attack was brief and violent, lasting a little over two minutes. The shots, screams and explosions quickly swallowed up by the chaos of a busy Colaba evening, the assailants walked out unchallenged. They bagged their Kalashnikovs and headed towards the Taj Mahal Palace and Tower that loomed behind. En route, they fished a small bag out of their haversack and placed it in a bylane near Gokul, another popular restaurant nearby. The two young men walked on until they reached the Northcote Gate, at the side of the Taj.

21.38 hours / Taj Palace

Abu Rehman Bada (alias Hafiz Arshad) and Abu Ali (alias Javed) had meanwhile emerged from their taxi near the Gateway of India after slipping a timed explosive device under the driver's seat. They entered the fragrant, opulent lobby of the Taj Mahal Palace with its faraway tinkle of music and unhurried sybaritic buzz. Hafiz and Javed could have passed off for any of the several backpacking tourists in the hotel. They glided into the lobby and turned left into a granite-lined corridor, flanked by a Louis Vuitton store and the hotel reception counter manned by the courteous, impeccably attired saree-clad executives. The corridor led deep into the old wing. The 5'10"-tall and well-built Hafiz, sporting a red baseball hat, stopped halfway down the corridor and pulled an AK-47 out of the bag, calmly inserted a pair of magazines and cocked his weapon. Javed followed his lead.

N.N. Krishnadas, a Communist Party of India (Marxist) member of Parliament from northern Kerala's Palakkad constituency was halfway through his dinner at the Shamiana restaurant, by the Taj poolside, behind the main lobby. He first heard a firecracker-like sound, followed by the crash of cutlery and then screams as diners fell to the floor. Krishnadas was with three other lawmakers – Jaisingh Gaikwad of the Nationalist Congress Party (NCP), Lal Mani Prasad of the Bahujan Samaj Party (BSP) and Bhupendra Singh Solanki of the Bharatiya Janata Party (BJP). They were part of a parliamentary delegation that was being hosted in the hotel and were the largest group of Indians in the restaurant. Krishnadas saw a gun-wielding terrorist outside. He didn't enter the restaurant. Hafiz and Javed walked away, firing from the hip into the elevator area and killing guests lounging by the poolside.

Hafiz's bullets crackled wildly down the shiny granite corridors and towards Shoaib and Nazir who strolled into the hotel from the Northcote entrance. Instinctively, the duo spun around and split to take cover behind pillars. The two terrorists, relieved at their narrow escape, emerged from their cover and walked down to team up with Hafiz and Javed at the bank of elevators in the lobby of the Taj Palace. Their timing was impeccable. The four then rode an elevator to the sixth floor of the hotel's heritage section, leaving twenty bodies on the ground floor.

Priya Florence Martis, twenty-one, mistook these shots fired for firecrackers from the wedding reception on at the hotel that night. She had just finished her second month as data centre executive at the Taj Palace, and barely knew her way around the maze of rooms. This was her first job and she had come in three hours early to relieve a colleague. She took her workstation in the server room of the Taj on the second floor overlooking the poolside. The room was a converted guest bedroom. It was one of the most vital spaces within the hotel. Inside, floor-to-ceiling IBM servers streamed and backed up data from the Taj Group's ninety-three hotels, fifty-five in India and the others abroad. The office was located directly beneath the grand dome of the hotel. The shots continued. Then an explosion reverberated through the hotel. She received a frantic call from her father Faustine Martis, a head steward in the hotel. 'Priya,' he said, anxiously, 'the hotel is under attack. Stay where you are, I will come and get you.'

Between 10.30 and 10.40 p.m., two taxis exploded on Mumbai's streets. The first vehicle blew up on the Western Express at Vile Parle near the domestic airport showering the road with the body parts of its driver Umar Shaikh and passenger, Laxminarayan Goyal, an advocate who had hired the taxi from CST station; the other at Mazgaon, 3 km north of CST station killed its driver Fulchand Bhind and his passengers, Zarina Sheikh and her daughter Reema. A fog of war enveloped Mumbai. Panic swept across the city. False alarms were reported from various hotels. The massacre of the police officers only added fuel to the fire. The rumours were that sixty terrorists had attacked the city. Panic-stricken Mumbaikars made 267 calls to the police control room between 9.40 p.m. and 2 a.m. Two calls said that the police commissioner's office was under attack.

The siege of Mumbai had begun: an audacious operation planned with military precision and ruthlessly executed within a tight three-square-kilometre box in the jugular of India's commercial capital. The GPS handsets that the buddy pairs carried had pre-fed way points locating their targets. It enabled the five teams to navigate efficiently on alien terrain.

In a Lashkar-e-Taiba (LeT) mission control room specially set up for the purpose near Karachi's tony residential area, Malir Cantonment, five LeT handlers – Sajid Mir, Abu Qahafa, Abu Alqama, Zarar Shah and Zabiuddin Ansari – were at work. They were wearing headsets and speaking Urdu and Punjabi into the Internet telephone connections on four laptops to motivate and direct the five buddy pairs. The Lashkar's control room also had TV sets tuned to various Indian news channels. The information communication revolution had transformed the world. It would now, in an unprecedented way, help trans-border terrorist masterminds exercise military-style command and control for the duration of the attack.

In the heritage wing of the Taj, Priya Martis instinctively locked the door of her office, switched the lights off and rushed into the small supervisor's cabin. She ducked under the table and pulled the supervisor's intercom into the space with her. The intercom was connected to all fifteen phones in her office. She was frightened by what she saw. The room had clear glass doors and windows. She was hiding in a glasshouse. A few hours later, she saw the outline of a man hammering the glass door. He was armed. She retreated further under the table, furiously praying, her face a mask of tension. The hammering stopped. He moved away. Then she heard shots, explosions and screams as the terrorists gunned down the guests. She prayed furiously. She choked and gasped as smoke from the hotel fires rolled down the ventilation shafts.

Meanwhile, DCP Vishwas Nangre-Patil and five policemen had entered the hotel through the Northcote entrance. They were guided into the southern wing of the heritage section by the hotel's security manager, Sunil Kudiyadi. Patil and his team were armed with service revolvers, pistols and two rifles. They exchanged sporadic fire with the terrorists, and entered the close-circuit TV (CCTV) control room of the hotel, located on the second floor. It was shortly after midnight. From here, the policemen helplessly monitored the havoc all around.

The gunmen broke into the hotel suites and rounded up four hostages, bound their hands and marched them into Room 632. This sea-facing suite became their operations base for the next two hours. They spoke with their handlers and combed the sixth floor for more hostages. Mumbai police vans called 'assault mobiles' and quick reaction teams had already converged on the hotel, but did not move in. For two critical hours, the police watched, helpless. Over a hundred policemen, many of them armed with assault rifles, had converged at the Taj, but they were not pushed in to corner the terrorists. 'The MARCOS [Marine Commandos] should be there in a few minutes. Keep them pinned down,' Police Commissioner Hasan Gafoor advised Patil on the wireless.

But the four terrorists were not going to wait. Working on instructions from their Karachi-based handlers, who suspected the police were monitoring the hotel CCTV cameras, they soaked upholstery and carpets with alcohol and set them ablaze. The cameras were destroyed. The security forces were blinded. Television channels relayed images of tongues of flame licking the red onion dome of the southern corner of the Taj. The handlers were overjoyed. 'My brother, yours is the most important target. *Sabse zyadaa apke target ko* coverage *de rahi hai* media,' chuckled Abu Alqama. Live television coverage added a dramatic twist to the siege. It allowed the handlers to assess the impact of their actions in real time. Television was both a medium and an unwitting messenger for the handlers. Soon after midnight, Indian

TV channels flashed phone-ins with the MPs trapped in the Taj. They had rashly narrated their plight and revealed their location: The Chambers, a members-only club situated on the mezzanine floor between the hotel lobby and the tower.

The MPs were not alone. There were over a hundred other guests, many of whom had come to attend a wedding reception in the Crystal Room. The handlers got to work. At 3.10 a.m., one of the LeT's handlers called one of the four terrorists rampaging through the hotel.

Terrorist: Greetings!

Handler: Greetings! There are three ministers and secretary of the cabinet in your hotel. We don't know in which room.

Terrorist: Oh that is good news. It is the icing on the cake.

Handler: Find those persons and get whatever you want from India.

Terrorist: Pray that we find them.

Handler: Do one thing, throw one or two grenades on the navy and police teams which are outside.

The terrorists set out in search of potential hostages through the hotel.

22.00 Hours / The Oberoi–Trident

Fahadullah and Abdul Rehman Chhota abandoned their rubber boat on the rocks at Nariman Point, where the Marine Drive promenade ended abruptly in the Arabian Sea, and hailed a taxi. Their destination stood less than half a kilometre away. The taxi drove down a tree-lined avenue illuminated with the orange glow of sodium vapour street lamps, past the National Centre for Performing Arts (NCPA) and the uptown NCPA apartments, and up the steep driveway of the Trident, where it discharged its passengers. Fahadullah and Chhota had already pulled out their AK-47s. They first shot at the Gucci showroom that stood to the left of the driveway, killing a security guard. As staffers fled and hid for cover, the duo walked down and placed a plastic bag at the foot of the driveway. They then announced their entry into the hotel with a hail of bullets that shattered the glass doors. They walked over the glass and past the black granite–topped concierge desk, casually spraying lead around the lobby, killing nine fleeing Oberoi staffers and three guests. One of them was thirty-eight year old Japanese businessman Hisashi Tsuda. He had exited an elevator near the reception and walked into the path of the two gunmen. He turned and fled towards the elevators. The terrorists fatally wounded him before he ran back.

Fahadullah and Chhota then climbed a flight of black granite steps which led to the twenty-one-storey Oberoi Hotel. They fired short bursts into the glass-fronted shops that lined the corridor. They strode into the Tiffin, a restaurant in the lower lobby, and then to the lounge area, where they left another plastic bag containing an IED.

Pradeep Bengalorkar ignored the shots. He had spent thirty years in the hotel and had been through hundreds of lavish weddings where Dom Perignon flowed like water, the baraat burst crackers on the Marine Drive and launched bottle rockets into the skies. The bespectacled fifty-one-year-old waiter at the Kandahar restaurant on the second floor, the pool level, was serving a tray of piping hot seekh kababs to one of the guests by the large sea-facing windows. Pradeep wore a cream-coloured shalwar and a baggy kurta, a brown jacket and black shoes. It was a busy night; each one of the twenty-three tables in south Mumbai's most popular Mughlai restaurant were occupied. The eleven restaurant staff had their hands full. Pradeep was the oldest staffer on duty that evening. The youngest, Jordan Fernandes, twenty-two, walked about with a spring in his step. The lean, athletically built assistant steward was serving out his last four days on duty and had told Pradeep he was looking forward to his new job in an Australian hotel. The lone tabla player sat on the elevated wooden platform, immersed in his performance.

Then, the din of cracker-like sounds started approaching the 1,000-square-foot restaurant. The tabla player stopped his recital. The shots were followed by piercing shrieks. Heads turned away from companions and dinner plates towards the door where the shots came from. Some diners started heading towards the exit. Pradeep and the other restaurant staff walked towards the door. They saw a terrifying sight at the Tiffin, a level below. Two gunmen shot people as they crouched under the tables. Single shots to the head. At point blank range. Pradeep recoiled and ran back inside. 'Stay inside the restaurant,' he told the diners, 'you are safe here.'

The restaurant staff thought these were underworld assassins who would kill and leave. But, to their horror, the gunmen didn't stop. Pradeep saw them sprint up the granite stairs that led to the Kandahar. The gunmen stopped at the spa next door and calmly shot the petite Thai receptionist who manned the counter. The Kandahar was next. 'I'm leading the guests out of the service exits,' Rahul Kadam, the young restaurant manager told his staff. He hastened the diners out towards the long corridor to one side of the restaurant entrance. Pradeep and Jordan Fernandes saw a few diners hiding under the tables.

'They're killing people hiding under the tables,' Pradeep hissed at them, 'let's get out.' The two stewards pushed the dozen remaining diners out through the narrow corridor: 'go, go ... run away from here'. Fahadullah and Chhota were just a few feet away from joining them when they heard a shout. '*Ruk jao*,' Fahadullah said, *'varna goli chalaoonga.'* Pradeep and Jordan froze. The last guest that Pradeep had pushed inside turned around in the corridor, away from the gaze of the terrorists. He gestured for Pradeep to join them. But the two stewards were transfixed. They turned around. Fahadullah stood holding an AK-47 levelled in his hand. He was of medium height, around five feet eight inches tall, dressed in a black shirt and black trousers. He wore brown sneakers and carried a haversack on his shoulder. The fingers of his left hand, curled around the rifle grip, were wrapped in a green cloth. His partner Abdul stood behind, he was shorter and dressed almost identically. If Fahadullah and Abdul Rehman were mildly amused to see how the stewards were dressed, they didn't show it. They had other uses for the two. The gunmen jerked their assault rifles towards a wine trolley and asked the stewards to set fire to the dining tables. Pradeep was to soak the tables with liquor, Jordan was to set fire to them.

The stewards, still believing these men were gangsters, complied reluctantly. 'The underworld has become terribly violent,' Pradeep thought to himself as he emptied the contents of a bottle of red wine onto a table. The choice of wine was deliberate. It would not burn. The two stewards grinned at each other, silently delighted in their mischief. The gunmen clearly did not know their alcohol. *'Aag lagao,'* Fahadullah shouted at Jordan who struggled with the matchbox. The gunmen ensured the stewards never came closer than six feet, motioning them away with their rifles and shouting '*door raho, door raho*' if they came any closer. The stewards ran out of matchboxes. '*Jaldi karo, jaldi karo*,' Fahadullah shouted, then picked up a cloth serviette and threw it at him. '*Isko aag lagao*.' As Jordan fumbled and lit the napkin from one of the burning tables, it caught fire and burnt his hand. '*Haath jalgaya na*,' he grimaced. Fahadullah's response was two AK-47 shots. Two bullets hit Jordan in the chest and left eye and shattered the large sea-facing glass window. The young waiter keeled over, dead. Pradeep felt real fear for the first time that evening. He set the tables on fire. The bluish flame on the wine-soaked table was quickly doused when the hotel's fire-fighting system kicked in.

The terrorists cursed. They had lost fifteen minutes in the restaurant. They were in a hurry. '*Bas ho gaya*,' Fahadullah shouted. '*Baahar chalo. Oopar le chalo aur batao kaun kaun-se* VIPs *hain*. (Come out. Take us upstairs and tell us who are the VIPs.)'

Pradeep tried feverishly to distract them. He led the way out of the restaurant. 'They killed Jordan because they didn't need him any more,' he thought to himself. 'They will kill me once I lead them upstairs.' He had to find a way to buy time and plan his escape. A set of elevators outside the restaurant led to the lobby level two floors below. Pradeep led them to it.

'Oye,' Fahadullah shouted when he saw the elevator arrow pointing downwards. *'Oopar jaana hai humein, neeche nahin.'*

Pradeep explained these elevators would take them downstairs, from where they would have to take another elevator. *'Hum to* restaurant *mein kaam karte hain* … hamey pata nahin; *oopar ka samajh nahin hai* … (I work in the restaurant, I don't know about the upper floors)' he babbled. It was a lie. He knew the hotel like the back of his hand and had worked in every department of the hotel, from banquets to room service.

Then Fahadullah saw people milling about in the dark reception area. *'Abdul, do gola phenk do, sab bhaag jayenge.'* Chhota placed his rifle on the floor and knelt. Fahadullah placed his AK-47 on the floor to fish grenades out of his companion's haversack. This was Pradeep's moment. As the terrorists flung the two bombs into the lobby, Pradeep darted inside the elevator and slammed the button that read 'Lower Lobby'. The brass-clad doors began to slide shut. Fahadullah turned around and fired two shots at his escaping hostage. One bullet hit the brass door. The second hit the wall. The doors closed. Pradeep had escaped.

At around 10.15 p.m., the IED that the terrorists had planted at the driveway went off. It punched a hole in the Trident's boundary wall and tossed aside a bomb blanket that the police had placed over it. The shock wave shattered the Trident's twelve-foot-high glass panes in the lobby, uprooted a palm tree and smashed vehicles parked outside. Fifteen minutes later, a second IED placed in the lobby of the Oberoi detonated. Fortunately, it had been left behind a pillar and that absorbed most of the shock wave. But the impact shook the building and the invisible wave reverberated through the atrium, blowing out all the glass on the lobby floors. The sofas in the Tea Lounge, a scenic sit-out by the lobby, caught fire. Thick black smoke billowed out and filled the atrium.

Commander Sushil Nagmote took cover behind a table as the hotel edifice shook. The hotel's chief security officer had rushed there from his flat in Cuffe Parade as soon as he got a frantic call from his assistant close to 10 p.m. informing him of a blast. The twin explosions only confirmed the retired naval officer's fears after he had followed the trail of violence, blood, bodies and shattered glass. The hotel was under an unprecedented terrorist attack. A diner lay slumped in a chair in the lobby's open-air restaurant, his intestines spilling out. A police inspector fired hesitant single shots from his pistol towards the elevated flight of stairs that led to the Oberoi. A constable pointed his self-loading rifle and fired aimlessly in the same direction. Nagmote now frantically tried to minimize casualties. He urgently instructed the engineers to shut down the elevators and prevent guests from pouring into the lobby area.

Fahadullah and Abdul Rehman had by now used the guest elevators to go up to the twelfth floor of the Oberoi, looking for hostages. As they emerged, they ran into a group of fifteen diners who had escaped their bullets in the Kandahar. In a cruel twist, the survivors had walked straight back to their tormentors. The terrorists rounded them up and walked them to the twenty-first floor, firing shots at the ceiling to hurry them up. On that floor, the service stairs telescoped into a narrow stairwell that led to the hotel's elevator machinery rooms. Ten of the hostages were lined up against the wall and shot. Five hostages, including four women, were taken downstairs. Among them were a Turkish couple Seyfi Muezzinoglu and her husband Meltam and Lo Hwei Yen, a twenty-eight-year-old Singaporean lawyer. She had travelled to Mumbai earlier that day to deliver a talk on the impact of the credit crunch on the shipping industry and was at a dinner in the Kandahar when the terrorists struck. She had fled upstairs into the hotel. Now, she was part of the last five survivors who were taken to room 1979 where the terrorists debated their fate.

At around 3.30 a.m., Yen called her husband, Michael Puhaindran, in Singapore. She now relayed the terrorists' message: 'Get the Singapore government to tell the Mumbai authorities to refrain from storming the hotel, or else she would lose her life.' Soon after, she called her husband one last time. Her voice was calm but firm: 'Please tell them (the authorities) to hurry up.'

At close to 4 a.m., Abdul Rehman received a call from two of his handlers in the LeT's control room in Karachi.

Handler: Brother Abdul, the media is comparing your action to 9/11. One senior police officer has been killed.

Abdul Rehman: We are on the tenth or eleventh floor. We have five hostages.

Handler 2/ Abu Kahafa: Everything is being recorded by the media. Inflict the maximum damage. Keep fighting. Don't be taken alive.

Handler 1: Kill all hostages, except the two Muslims. Keep your phone switched on so that we can hear the gunfire.

Fahadullah: We have three foreigners, including women from Singapore and China.

Handler 1: Kill them.

Fahadullah and Abdul Rehman then directed the Turkish couple to stand aside. The confined space reverberated with the sound of gunfire.

22.25 Hours / Nariman House

Babar Imran, who used the code name Abu Akasha, and Abu Umar strode towards Chabad House using a narrow pedestrian path that linked Colaba Causeway to

Captain Prakash Pethe Marg. They crossed the crowded twenty-foot-wide causeway where furiously snorting Brihanmumbai Electric Supply and Transport (BEST) buses passed each other, aluminium sides practically scraping. Colaba was filled as usual with the tinny sounds of hundreds of honking vehicles inching past shops and pedestrians. They stopped by the Express Petrol station and placed an IED under a vehicle.

The two men then turned around the corner and walked up the three steps, all that was left of what fishermen called 'paanch pairi' (five steps), that led to the narrow Hormusji Street, newly paved with interlocking red tiles. Imran and Nasir homed in on a building tucked down it. It had a prominent steel glow sign in white and cyan that said 'Chabad House' in English and Hebrew.

The cream-coloured building had been bought in 2006 by Gavriel Holtzberg, twenty-nine, and his wife Rivka. It was built where an old colonial bungalow had once stood. The Holtzbergs worked for the Brooklyn-based Chabad Liberation Movement for Hasidic Jews, an ultra-orthodox movement that provided a home and prayer services for Jewish travellers in sixty-five countries worldwide. Gasvriel and Livka were among thousands of 'emissary families' that worked in the world's largest Jewish network.

Babar Imran and Nasir walked up the stairs to the second floor of the house renamed after a Hebrew acronym for *chochmah* (wisdom), *binah* (comprehension) and *da'at* (knowledge). They blasted their way into the flat and almost immediately executed three Jewish house guests, including sixty-year-old Israeli tourist Yocheved Orpaz, twenty-eight-year-old American-Israeli national Bentzion Chroman and his friend, the Chabad House's kosher supervisor, thirty-seven-year old Rabbi Leibisch Teitelbaum. The terrorists then took four hostages: the Holtzbergs and their son Moshe and a fifty-year-old house guest, Norma Rabinovich. Meanwhile, the Holtzbergs' cook Zakir, nicknamed Jackie, and their son's nanny, Sandra Samuel, cowered in the pantry on the first floor.

Santosh Dattaram Veer, a thirty-one-year-old Shiv Sena worker, had his eyes focused on the TV set. He was cheering India's win in the cricket match when he heard the sound of gunfire. 'Somebody's celebrating,' he thought to himself as he lounged about on the terrace of Sarabhai House. The roof of the single-storeyed tenement had a 100-square-foot makeshift office of a local Ganesh utsav mandal. There were more shots. Then screams. They came from the direction of Nariman House.

Santosh and five friends, including Harish Gohil, ran towards the building. The watchman had disappeared. The youth ran upstairs. Santosh saw the Holtzbergs' cook Jackie, who frantically shouted, *'Bhaago, bhaago'*. Santosh and his friends ran up to the third floor. Just over the staircase, he saw one of the terrorists with an AK-47. He did not look like an Israeli. Something was wrong. *'Oopar aao, oopar aao,'* the terrorist challenged them. The youths backed off and ran downstairs.

Smoke billowed out of Chabad House. The crowd saw the figure of Rabbi Gavriel Holtzberg silhouetted against the light. There was something amiss. Through the iron grille that covered the window, they saw Holtzberg silently motioning the crowd with both his hands as if to say 'move back'. Suddenly, a grenade bounced down and exploded, showering deadly steel shrapnel around the building. A terrorist appeared on the window where the rabbi had just stood, poked a gun barrel out and raked the street with gunfire. One of the bullets hit Harish Gohil in the chest. He died on his way to the hospital.

The locals of Colaba regarded their Jewish neighbours with mild curiosity when they first arrived two years ago. Now, they believed they had unleashed hidden weapon caches on them. 'It's these foreigners ... they're drunk and they've fired their guns,' builder and former Congress party corporator Puran Doshi seethed as he led a crowd of irate locals towards the building. The crowd beat up a foreigner fleeing the Chabad House. It was fifty-two-year-old Antwerp-based diamond merchant David Bialka, who had escaped the slaughter. The youth then directed their ire at the building. They uprooted paving stones and hurled it at the building but quickly retreated when the terrorists reappeared and shot at them. An IED the terrorists had planted at a petrol pump behind the building exploded. A few minutes later, terrorists set off another IED on the ground floor. The explosion bent the iron sliding gate, a portion of the wall on the first floor collapsed inwards and left a heap of bricks on the garage floor. The residents fled.

'Civilians are easier to kill,' the scholar C. Douglas Lummins noted in a seminal essay on the military. 'Untrained, unorganized and unarmed, they don't know how to take cover, don't act according to a plan, and can't shoot back. It is much more dangerous to try and kill soldiers; you might get killed yourself.'

The trained soldiers who could respond quickest to this emergency were, ironically, located at the southern end of Colaba Causeway, less than 2 km away. Col Arun 'Aries' Sharma's ear cocked up when he heard the distant yet distinctive rattle of an AK-47. Sharma, commanding officer of the 2nd battalion of the Grenadiers, hadn't heard that sound since he left the Kashmir Valley three years back. Hearing the rattle, he came out of his spacious colonial bungalow at 10 Duxbury Lane just 2 km away from Nariman House.

TV news channels breathlessly spoke of a gang war that was on in Colaba. But there was something about these shots that troubled Sharma. The gunfire came in short precise bursts: the discipline that comes from firing hundreds of rounds in training. It told the veteran of a dozen firefights with militants all that he needed to know. 'These are no gangsters,' he thought to himself. 'The local police can't cope with this.' He headed back inside to retrieve his mobile phone and call his officers who were in a party in the unit mess. Sharma's 800-strong infantry battalion housed in the Colaba garrison had spent seven straight years in counter-insurgency operations before coming to Mumbai in 2007. Two days ago, they had returned from a major exercise in the Rajasthan desert. Tonight, he thought, he saw a return to action. 'Get ready boys,' he said into his cellphone. 'We will be called at some point.'

The Army, NSG and Marcos Are Called In

Maharashtra's Chief Secretary Johny Joseph had begun to receive frantic calls on his cellphone from around 9.50 p.m. The fifty-nine-year-old Joseph, who joined the Indian Administrative Service in 1972, had only just returned to his fourteenth-floor residence in Sarang building. The apartment was less than 200 metres from his office in the state secretariat, Mantralaya, and just half a kilometre north of the road the eight terrorists had landed on an hour before. Joseph still sported his trademark dark-blue safari suit. When the TV images suggested an emergency, an ashen-faced Joseph rushed to his waiting vehicle and returned to his office. On 26 July 2005, Mumbai's suburbs had been deluged and Joseph, then municipal commissioner, was severely criticized for not responding in time.

Joseph's office was on the fifth floor of the Soviet-style secretariat. It was adjacent to the state government's control room that had been set up after the 1993 Latur earthquake. Joseph's first call was to Chief Minister Vilasrao Deshmukh, away in Kerala, requesting him to immediately return to the city. The chief secretary then rushed into his office at around 10 p.m. and mobilized his crisis management team comprising all important state government secretaries. Twenty minutes after Joseph had entered his office, it became clear that Mumbai was under a massive terrorist attack. Terrorists with sophisticated weapons and grenades had attacked multiple locations, Police Commissioner Hasan Gafoor told him. Gafoor had instructed one of his joint commissioners, Rakesh Maria, to man the control room in police headquarters at Crawford Market. As head of the state bureaucracy, Joseph decided to supplement relief efforts.

Meanwhile, Dr Chandrakant Gaikwad, the medical superintendent of the state-owned St George's Hospital, called. The hospital was located right behind CST. He was frantic. Bodies were arriving by the cart load, he told

Joseph. 'They're not injured,' Dr Gaikwad said. 'They're just dead.'

There had been attacks at seven places. The terrorists had entered the Taj, the Trident, Cama Hospital and Nariman House. The situation was grim. Around 10.30 p.m., Joseph received a call from New Delhi. It was Cabinet Secretary K.M. Chandrasekhar, the country's most powerful bureaucrat. A phone call from him could set the wheels of government moving long after office hours. Joseph asked him to send in the National Security Guard (NSG). India's Constitution mandates law and order to be a state subject. The Central government stays away unless its assistance is specifically sought. Chandrasekhar waived the formalities aside. 'I will personally ensure they are dispatched to Mumbai,' he assured Joseph.

In the meantime, more worrying news started pouring in. Terrorists had taken hostages. Civilians had been killed and seriously injured. The situation appeared to be slipping out of the hands of the police. The NSG wouldn't reach for a few hours yet. Joseph needed army commandos. 'This is war,' Joseph thought to himself as he dialled Major General R.K. Hooda, the general officer commanding (GOC), Maharashtra, Gujarat and Goa area.

Major General Hooda lived in the Colaba military area less than 3 km south of Mantralaya in the imposing

'Gun House'. The name was an overstatement. The only soldiers the general commanded were in peacetime establishments – the base workshops, hospitals and offices – in the three coastal states. The 2 Grenadiers unit reported to the Pune-based Southern Army Command. 'Send me commandos,' Joseph said frantically. The general informed him that he did not have any, the army having deployed them in Jammu and Kashmir. The GOC, however, offered to send in his army columns. Joseph then dialled his friend, Rear Admiral M.P. Muralidharan, the navy's flag officer, Maharashtra Area. The admiral told him that the navy had commandos on a base in the mainland across the harbour. Delighted with this news, the chief secretary immediately dialled Rear Admiral R.K. Pattanaik, chief of staff and the de facto number two of the Mumbai-based Western Naval Command. Pattanaik agreed to dispatch the MARCOS at the earliest. A harbour craft, a 100-foot-long passenger boat that ferried passengers between the naval dockyard and the mainland, set sail at 11 p.m. to fetch the commandos. At 11.20 p.m., Joseph received a call from Rakesh Maria, manning the police control room, that confirmed his worst fears. 'We cannot control this, sir,' Maria said.

The army had to be called in. It took the army another hour to agree to send troops to the locations.

At 12.35 a.m. on 27 November, Lt General Amarjit Singh Sekhon, the Delhi-based director general, Military

Operations (DGMO), cleared the deployment of five army columns to assist the local administration. By 1 a.m., the men of the 2 Grenadiers had boarded trucks and moved out of their barracks in south Mumbai. An hour later, at 2 a.m., nearly 800 soldiers ringed the Leopold Café, Taj Palace and Tower, Oberoi Hotel, the CST station and Cama Hospital. The terrorists, meanwhile, rampaged through the Taj and Oberoi, hunting their victims down with cold-blooded efficiency.

Since the start of the insurgency in Jammu and Kashmir in 1989, all of the Indian Army's 350-odd infantry battalions had been deployed in counter-insurgency operations. The 'Grinders' as they were called, had spent nearly a decade in J&K. In 1994, it had received a unit citation for killing 150 terrorists in a single year. Since then, the unit's personnel had killed over 200 foreign terrorists or FTs, as the army called Pakistani and Afghan terrorists. Tonight, however, the 2 Grenadiers waited for orders to enter the locations. Col Sharma, meanwhile, waited in Colaba with his 'Ghatak' platoon, twenty-four of his finest soldiers, the tip of the 2 Grenadiers' spear. If the order came, these men would storm the hotels and engage the terrorists. But the order never came.

'NSG ko bulao'

The phones had already begun ringing in the national capital. But the government did not convene a meeting of the National Crisis Management Committee (NCMC). The NCMC, headed by the cabinet secretary included sixteen key government secretaries. Instead, the Union government's responses flowed in bureaucratic fashion, through the lumbering home ministry. The Ministry of Home Affairs (MHA) maintained internal security but stepped in only when states were unable to respond to a crisis. The internal security establishment was only one of twenty-four major departments that, among other things, gathered intelligence, fought terrorism, policed borders, seized drugs, dispensed funds to modernize state police forces, paid freedom fighter pensions, handled immigration, created new states and appointed governors. It also ran training programmes and poster campaigns to promote the national language, Hindi.

Home Secretary Madhukar Gupta who administered this mammoth ministry, was in Islamabad for talks with his Pakistani counterpart Syed Kamal Shah. He had crossed over to Lahore from the Wagah border just two days earlier. Gupta carried with him a list of thirty-two Indian and ten Pakistani fugitives wanted for terrorist offences in India, which he handed over to Shah. The list included the 1993 bombing suspects Memon and Dawood and Maulana Masood Azhar, wanted for the December 2001 attacks on India's parliament. Just hours before the Mumbai massacre, Gupta had issued a joint statement with Shah that condemned terrorism and affirmed their resolve to end the menace. Both sides also welcomed the release of fishermen captured by their coastguards as they breached the international boundary. The irony of this statement would strike them much later. With Gupta away, at about 10 p.m., Home Minister Shivraj Patil dialled the second most important person in his ministry, Mahendra Lal Kumawat, special secretary, Internal Security (SSIS). 'See if they need any help,' Patil told him.

Kumawat was the most overworked policeman in the country that night. In addition to his duties as SSIS, he also held charge as director general of the 200,000-strong Border Security Force (BSF) that guarded borders with Pakistan and Bangladesh; he was also director general of the Narcotics Control Bureau (NCB), another vacant post that was yet to be filled. He attended over six meetings a day and was often briefed as he walked through the sandstone corridors of North Block. Kumawat knew which of the 700,000 men in the MHA's seven paramilitaries was best suited for the task. It would be the force, which, the MHA's annual reports noted, was 'modelled on the SAS of the United Kingdom and the GSG-9 of Germany'. Kumawat dialled the NSG's director general, Jyoti Krishan Dutt, and instructed him to take his forces to Mumbai.

Dutt, in turn, dialled Major General Abhay Gupta, his inspector general (IG) in charge of NSG operations. The general, however, was in Mussoorie, the Himalayan hill station nearly 300 km north of the capital. He was to deliver a lecture on the NSG at the Lal Bahadur Shastri National Academy of Administration that trained India's civil servants. The cold war between Dutt and Gupta was the NSG's worst kept secret. But tonight, there was no hint of tension when they spoke. 'Please come back as soon as you can,' Dutt said.

The police officer had quickly realized that the 'shooting in Mumbai' his daughter had spoken of at the dinner table was no film shoot. As Dutt walked to the TV set and scrawls of 'gang war' appeared across the TV screen, his face creased into a frown. 'This is no gang war,' Dutt said to himself as he reached for his cellphone again.

Dutt dialled Brigadier Rangi, who commanded the Special Action Groups in Manesar as force commander. Rangi was on leave and outside the city. Next, he dialled the DIG (Operations and Training), Brigadier Govind Sisodia – the next officer in line – and asked him to ready his commandos.

'How many?' Sisodia asked.

'How many will fit in an IL-76?' Dutt wanted to know.

'Around 200,' Sisodia said.

'Then get them ready.'

With his senior commanders unlikely to return in time, Dutt decided to personally accompany his men to Mumbai.

Dutt then called Sanjeev Tripathi, the head of the Aviation Research Centre (ARC). The NSG depended on the ARC, the air arm of the Research and Analysis Wing (R&AW), to fly its commandos. The aircraft was available, Tripathi told him, but it had to be refuelled and the crew brought from home.

As Dutt drove towards the Delhi airport, his thoughts flashed back to the December 2006 meeting of the cabinet secretariat. He had proposed four NSG hubs in Mumbai, Kolkata, Chennai and Bangalore, manned by over 200 NSG personnel each. This was because Delhi airport became fog-bound in winter. It would be difficult to fly out the NSG at short notice. The hubs would reduce reaction time to a crisis. Dutt's proposal was vigorously opposed by home ministry bureaucrats who worried about financial implications. The multi-centre hub proposal was finally watered down to a single hub. In Kolkata. Even that proposal was 'under the consideration' of a subcommittee since January 2007. In short, put in cold storage.

Deadly Headley

On 11 November 1977, the Fatah faction of the Palestine Liberation Organization (PLO) launched yet another amphibious assault on Israel. This time, eleven terrorists rode two Zodiacs to Israel's Mediterranean coast. At around noon, they landed on a beach near

Ma'agan Michael, roughly 80 km north of Tel Aviv, and walked a mile to the four-lane Coastal Highway. They were armed with Kalashnikovs, hand grenades, rocket-propelled grenades and was led by a female terrorist, Dalal Mughrabi. The group first gunned down American tourist Gail Rubin, who had seen them on the beach, then commandeered passing taxis and two buses and began the shooting and grenade-hurling spree, now called the Coastal Road Massacre. Thirty-seven Israelis, including thirteen children, were killed before Israeli police shot and killed nine of the eleven terrorists at a hastily erected roadblock 11 km north of Tel Aviv. The tourist bus that the terrorists had hijacked exploded in a fireball.

It was till then Israel's worst terror attack. Strangely, this was not the attack Khalil Al Wazir aka 'Abu Jihad' had planned. The PLO's military mastermind had sent his operatives from Lebanon to capture a luxury hotel in Tel Aviv, take hostages for a siege and demand the release of their comrades in Israeli captivity. The plan hit a hurdle in the azure waters of the Mediterranean Sea. Two terrorists drowned when one of the two rubber boats capsized; the remaining eleven lost their way and landed short of their target. The attacks failed to thwart peace talks between Israeli prime minister Menachem Begin and Egyptian president Anwar Sadat and only steeled the Jewish nation's resolve to act against Fatah.

The PLO's naval commando raid was not short on training, motivation and planning. Fortunately for the Israelis, the terrorists didn't have satellite images of urban areas, hand-held Global Positioning Systems to steer them to the targets and secure communication with their base in Lebanon. All they had were films of the Tel Aviv shoreline which they viewed at their training camps in Lebanon. By the early 1990s, these tools were commercially available: Global Positioning System handsets, satellite telephones and Google Earth satellite images of cities. But what terrorists still lacked was precise information on where exactly to land their boats and the layout of their targets.

Tactical difficulties were part of the reason the LeT did not plan a larger attack on Mumbai. Until September 2007, the LeT had planned a hit-and-run raid on guests at the Taj Mahal Palace. Two gunmen would infiltrate the city from the porous Indo-Nepal or the Indo-Bangladesh border, carry out their deadly task and then flee north towards Kashmir. But after March 2008, the LeT's plan for modest mayhem changed. The group now began to discuss multiple attacks using more than two attackers. The change in strategy came amidst tumult within the LeT and a strategic power shift within Pakistan. The LeT military chief Zakiur Rahman Lakhvi wanted a big operation to refocus his group's fight against its prime enemy, India, because his cadres were restless and wanted to fight US-led coalition forces in Afghanistan.

There was a power shift within the Pakistan army that had for decades waged a covert war against India. On 28 November 2007, in an unprecedented move, Pakistan's military dictator-turned-president General Pervez Musharraf handed the reins of the army to the inscrutable, chain-smoking director general of the ISI, General Ashfaq Parvez Kayani. Never in Pakistan's history had the head of its deep state, the ISI, gone on to control its most powerful institution. General Kayani had been commissioned into the army just four months before the December 1971 war with India carved an independent Bangladesh out of East Pakistan. Kayani was awarded the 'Tamgha-e-Istaqlal' medal for mobilizing the Pakistan army as DGMO during India's eight-month-long border build-up after the 2001 attack on India's parliament.

The February 2008 general elections brought in a civilian government led by Asif Ali Zardari's Pakistan People's Party that began impeachment proceedings against General Musharraf. By 18 August, Musharraf was forced out of office and into exile in London. His nine-year rule had ended. The Pakistan army may have been in the barracks, but its ISI and its proxy arm, the LeT, continued to plan mayhem. They had already planted a deep-cover operative in Mumbai for the past two years. David Coleman Headley, then forty-six, had arrived in Mumbai in September 2006 a clean-shaven Caucasian businessman who carried a brand new US passport. He hid the fact that until March that year he was called Daood Gilani and was half-Pakistani. He was in Mumbai ostensibly to open the branch of First World Immigration Services. The agency was only a cover for his real mission. Headley carried with him $25,000 given to him by Major Iqbal of the ISI for scouting targets in Mumbai. He quickly discovered that a tall, well-built, English-speaking, white male could operate with impunity in India.

Headley the double agent had heterochromatic eyes, a blue right eye and a dark-brown left eye, and swore by General George S. Patton's favourite line, 'No guts, no glory'; but he was an unlikely terrorist. The son of Syed Salim Gilani, a poet and diplomat posted at the Pakistan embassy in Washington and Serill Headley, the daughter of a wealthy Philadelphia family who worked as an embassy secretary, Headley spent his early years with his father in Pakistan, attending the Hasan Abdal Cadet College, a military school for boys in Punjab's Attock district.

Serill brought Headley back to the US in 1977. He lived with his mother in an apartment above a nightclub 'Khyber Pass' that she ran in Philadelphia with her Afghan-born husband. Headley worked as a manager in the club and later, ran a video rental store in New York.

Headley returned to Pakistan in the early 1980s. US investigative website ProPublica notes that in 1984, Headley was caught trying to smuggle heroin out of Pakistan's tribal areas. He used his friend Tahawwur Rana, then studying to be a Pakistani military doctor, as cover. The ruse failed. He was imprisoned but broke out of prison. In 1988, he was caught trying to smuggle 2 kg of heroin into the US from Frankfurt airport. He was tried, served four years in a US prison and then cut a deal with the Drug Enforcement Agency (DEA). He agreed to work for them as an informant. He used his deep links with drug gangs in the Af-Pak region to uncover drug smugglers in the US.

Post-9/11, when US intelligence agencies scrambled for information on al Qaeda that operated from Afghanistan and later from Pakistan's lawless tribal regions, Headley turned into a vital asset. In Lahore, however, Headley was slowly drawn towards the violent, virulent India-hating ideology of the LeT and its founder ideologue, Hafiz Muhammad Saeed. The drifter found his ideological moorings within an organization determined to bleed India.

By 2002, the DEA double agent had become a triple agent. Headley was now being trained as a militant separately by both ISI and LeT. He was almost unrecognizable in the salwar kameez, a traditional Afghan 'pakol' cap and a beard that touched his chest. He was trained in unarmed combat, intelligence-gathering techniques and the fine art of cultivating agents in the LeT headquarters in Muridke outside Lahore and in the mountains of Muzaffarabad in Pakistan-occupied Kashmir. He volunteered to fight in Kashmir, but at forty, was rejected for being too old. The LeT and the ISI evidently had a bigger, more important role for him in mind. Their belief was vindicated when, during a flurry of eight visits between India and Pakistan between 2006 and 2008, Headley convinced his handlers that a large-scale attack on Mumbai was possible.

The fastest, most secure route to infiltrate men and material was over the Arabian Sea.

The LeT timed the attacks for September 2008, after the fury of the south-west monsoon had abated. In April 2008, Headley took four boat rides around southern Mumbai, from near the Taj Mahal Palace, from Marine Drive and the Worli area. He was looking for the landing spot for the terrorists. On 12 April 2008, he found it in Machhimar Nagar in Cuffe Parade. It offered the shortest possible access to all the targets and was adjacent to a busy road from where taxis could be hailed. Headley hired a boat from the fishing colony and headed out into the sea. There, 6 km out into the sea, he punched a series of GPS waypoints into a yellow Garmin GPS handset given to him by the LeT.

He managed the recces despite a tumultuous personal life. In February 2007, during one of his nine trips between Mumbai and Pakistan to meet his LeT and ISI handlers, he met an attractive Moroccan national Faiza Outalha at a mutual friend's home in Lahore. Sparks flew between the spy and the medical student. They were married that month. Headley hid the marriage from his first wife Shazia, whom he married in 1999 and had four children with. In March 2007, he brought Faiza to Mumbai where they extensively recced the Taj Mahal Palace, which was then the only target of the strike. Headley always carried a Sony Ericsson phone given to him by the ISI with which he filmed elaborate videos of the interiors and the rooms.

There was a tearful spat at the Taj Mahal Palace over Headley's first wife and in December 2007, Faiza got into another altercation outside Headley's house in Lahore. He spent eight days in jail for assault. Faiza later breezed into the American embassy in Islamabad and told the US State Department's security bureau that her husband was an international drug peddler and a terror spy who had been going to India on a secret mission. It is not clear what came of this revelation.

Headley, meanwhile, had completed videographing and obtaining GPS waypoints for all the targets in Mumbai. It would allow gunmen who had never travelled out of Pakistan before to steer themselves to pre-selected targets without asking for directions. His extensive knowledge of the city allowed the LeT to focus its murderous gunmen on proximate targets. He ruled out a strike against Shiv Sena chief Bal Thackeray's home, Matoshree: the terrorists could not travel 15 km from Colaba to his home in suburban Bandra, he reasoned. He knew the Mumbai police could not withstand a military-style assault. 'Does it work?' he once joked with a policeman armed with a vintage 9 mm carbine at Siddhivinayak temple. He then turned to tell a friend that it was a World War II weapon.

When the terrorists finally struck Mumbai, Headley was at the Holiday Inn in Lahore. He received an SMS from Sajid Mir, then present at the LeT's Karachi-based control room, asking him to switch on the TV. A few hours later, he received a coded email from his Chicago-based wife Shazia. 'I am watching cartoons,' wrote the Chicago-based homemaker. 'Congratulations on your graduation.'

Meanwhile, in Mumbai, the police had paid a terrible price for the criminal neglect of its force. By 2 a.m. on 27 November, seventeen policemen had died and thirty-five were injured. The news that the NSG was being called in travelled through Mumbai. It injected a placebo into the shattered morale of the city.

The Mumbai police withdrew from the Taj, Oberoi and Nariman House locations and waited for backup to arrive from 1,400 km away. In doing so, it made another fatal mistake. They 'broke contact' and gave the desperadoes a respite. The attackers now had the upper hand and higher ground. They had a free run of their targets and could plan their defence.

MARCOS to the Rescue

Prashant Mangeshikar sat on the green carpeted floor of the Chambers, an exclusive club area on the first floor of the Taj Tower directly above the lobby, and looked at the tangle of limbs around the darkened room. The faces of nearly 150 guests huddled in the darkened room were lit by the glow of cell phones as they texted and spoke in hushed whispers, to the outside world. The room reverberated with the steady crack of bullets and grenade blasts. Less than two hours ago, Mangeshikar, a gynaecologist at the Bombay Hospital, his wife Tilu Mangeshikar, an anaesthetist, and their daughter Kalindi were at the wedding reception of their daughter's friends Amit and Varsha Thadani at the Crystal Room. The venue had a special significance for them. The Mangeshikars had hosted their reception here in 1971. The muted revelry was interrupted by the sounds of what some of them variously thought were fire crackers or construction work. Then, bullets shattered a glass door, forcing over a hundred guests to crouch under the tables. Three terrorists entered the room, fired shots and bolted away. After a brief, anxious wait, the guests were escorted away by Taj hotel staff, through a service corridor, into the dining hall of the Chambers. Hotel staff had unplugged the television sets inside and locked the doors. Their sole link with the world outside were their mobile phones.

It had helped that they were in the dining hall. The precise and efficient hotel staff plied the guests with a steady flow of sandwiches and crates of drinking water. The early text messages that streamed in on their mobile phones spoke of a gang war. This led most guests to believe their stay here was only an interlude. 'We are going to be out of here soon,' Bhisham Mansukhani, thirty one, a city-based journalist, told Dr Prashant Mangeshikar. Bhisham and his mother Indra were guests at the wedding reception at the Crystal Room. The two families took pictures of each other on phone cameras. But as the hours passed, the sounds of gunfire and explosions grew louder. The messages on their phones became more urgent, more frantic. The Taj was only one of several locations that had been targeted by terrorists. Several policemen had been killed and the upper floors of the Taj were ablaze. Anxiety set in, but there was no panic. They waited for deliverance.

At around midnight on 27 November, a harbour craft 'Vahini' arrived at the boat jetty of an Indian naval special forces base, INS *Abhimanyu*. The base was just eight kilometres off the city on the mangrove-fringed mainland. An imposing memorial a little distance away from the jetty, a fifteen-foot high bronze frogman's hand wielding a dagger, was framed against the orange glow of the Mumbai city skyline. The granite plaque beneath the memorial read 'We live by duty, honour, courage, valour'. The sixteen heavily armed men – Indian Navy Marine Commandos or MARCOS – who swore by this motto, filed into the ferry. They were armed with AK-47s and MP5 sub-machine guns and holstered 9 mm pistols on their thighs. Hand grenades bulged in the pouches of the black, bulletproof vests they wore over Indian army combat fatigues.

The base commander briefed his men on the jetty. The information was still coming in driblets, he told them, but it was clear that it was a coordinated attack on city hotels. 'Vahini' chugged away from where the MARCOS used to parachute into the sea in full diving rig, ride helicopter-launched Zodiacs (rubber boats) for coastal raids and crawl through mud with full combat loads. The commandos sat in the enclosed seating area of the passenger craft and checked their weapons. Every one of them had rotated through the Wular freshwater lake north of Srinagar where they prevented the infiltration of Pakistani militants. The craft headed towards the naval dockyard past rows of moored merchantmen anchored in the harbour, of the kind the MARCOS had been recently deployed to protect from Somali pirates, in the Gulf of Aden.

Now they braced themselves for operations on unfamiliar terrain: five-star hotels in the heart of the metropolis. The commandos reached INS *Angre,* the navy's administrative headquarters deep inside the naval dockyard where two senior officers were waiting for them – a Commodore who headed naval operations and a Commander in charge of special forces operations. The commandos were divided into two teams. One team of eight commandos would accompany the two officers to the Taj Mahal Palace and Tower, another team of eight, along with a dog squad and a three-member team comprising bomb disposal experts from the naval dockyard, were sent to the Trident–Oberoi which police said, had been bombed.

When the team of eight MARCOS arrived at the Taj at 2 a.m., fire brigade personnel were desperately trying to douse the flames on the sixth floor of the old wing of the Taj Mahal Palace. They could hear intermittent firing on the upper floors. The hotel driveway, however, was deserted – an unusual sight even at that hour. Three policemen and a few hotel staff stood in the desolate reception area. There were bloodstains, broken glass shards and a trail of empty brass 7.62 mm shells on the floor leading to the swimming pool.

One of the three policemen was K.L. Prasad, joint commissioner of police, law and order. He wore a khakhi-coloured bulletproof vest. The situation, he informed the MARCOS, was dire. Four terrorists had entered the hotel. 'They've inflicted heavy casualties on the hotel guests. We need your assistance.'

There was no time to lose. The first priority for the commandos was to understand the hotel layout, to know all the possible entries and exits. The hotel staff produced a layout. It was a densely packed blueprint on an A4-sized sheet. The marine commando officer leading the teams could make no sense of it, so he tucked it into the pocket of his combat fatigues. He directed his men to head for the CCTV security room that the police had abandoned a short while ago. From here, the MARCOS reasoned, they could assess the number of terrorists, their location and the weapons they carried.

Sunil Kudiyadi, the hotel's security manager, escorted them into the south wing of the Taj Palace. Kudiyadi, a tall strapping professional, was a picture of calm in the chaos around. He was dressed in his black suit and tie with a brass name-plate and carried a walkie-talkie with which he communicated with security staff. He accompanied the commandos up the stairs of the silent hotel. They took the stairs behind the main reception area to climb up to the sixth floor.

Smoke from the burning floors upstairs filled the

hotel and poured through the lobbies. There was no visibility. The commandos abandoned this approach.

On the second floor, the commandos were in for another disappointment. The CCTV room was ablaze and thick smoke poured out of it.

Meanwhile, a murmur of relief travelled around the densely packed Chambers. The hotel staff had begun taking guests out in small batches. The guests left in small groups of twos and fours, all of them escorted by the hotel's Executive Chef Hemant Oberoi and his kitchen staff. The first to leave were the law makers whom Bhisham Mansukhani had seen giving interviews to TV channels from inside the dining hall. The full impact of those revelations was yet to be felt. Egged on by their Pakistan-based handlers, the four terrorists had sprinted down from the top floors of the Taj Palace to search for prized VIP hostages on the first floor. The terrorists arrived after around fifty guests had moved down the narrow service corridors into the lobby. They now set upon the remaining guests who lined the corridor. There were screams and the rattle of gunfire. No one could see where the shots were coming from. The nervous but orderly file, disintegrated into a stampede. They turned and darted back into the function rooms that stood in the corridor beside the Chambers.

The MARCOS heard the staccato bursts of fire echoing down the corridors. 'They're coming from the direction of the kitchen area,' Kudiyadi exclaimed. The kitchen complex formed the second link between the heritage wing and the new Taj Tower. The team rushed towards it, guns at the ready. Kudiyadi showed them the way. The group cautiously approached the kitchen area. There was a sound that grew louder as they came closer. It was the trilling of dozens of cell phones: frantic, unanswered calls to the fifteen victims who lay contorted on the floor. Most of those victims were uniformed Taj staff, shot while fleeing, looking for cover. The green stone tiles were splattered with blood. At least seven persons were alive and seriously injured, writhing in pain on the floor. An injured lady was trapped beneath the corpse of a dead person. She looked at a commando and wailed weakly, 'Take her off me.'

The commandos tensed as they approached one of the kitchen doors. Three gunmen were walking past. They saw the MARCOS. One of them whirled around and fired a burst from his hip and threw a grenade. The commandos took cover. The grenade did not explode. The terrorists fled through the numerous exits from the kitchen. 'Evacuate the injured out of here,' the team leader whispered to Kudiyadi.

The firefight told the commandos that they were up against heavily armed terrorists. But they also came upon another realization. The hotel was full of civilians. The MARCOS were all specialists: in communications, sharp shooting and handling explosives. But now, in the labyrinthine maze of the dimly lit hotel, they needed only one speciality: nerves of steel. They could not afford to be trigger-happy. As the commandos began shifting the wounded out of the corridor. Their priority had swiftly changed from neutralizing the terrorists to evacuating civilians.

More commandos were needed. The task was simply too large for eight men, however well trained. They radioed their chief of operations in the hotel lobby for reinforcements as they began helping the wounded out of the corridors.

The civilians who had escaped the slaughter had by now barricaded themselves into the rooms around the Chambers. The Mangeshikars, Bhisham Mansukhani and his mother were among fifty-odd guests who found refuge in the Lavender Room, at the far end of the corridor. The guests broke off a chair leg and jammed it through the door handles and pushed a circular table and piled chairs against the door. Tilu Mangeshikar was relieved to see her husband Prakash and daughter Kalindi were safe inside with her. She, however, had an emergency to attend to. Rajan Kamble, a hotel maintenance worker, who had been shot while trying to escort the guests in the corridor. A bullet had drilled his back and tore his abdomen out as it exited. Despite the chaos, the guests managed to pull him inside their hideaway. Kamble's white uniform was blood soaked and his face contorted with pain. Tilu Mangeshikar used hotel serviettes to push his intestines back in. She laid the grievously wounded staffer on the floor and administered pain killers borrowed from a guest and when a table cloth would not hold his intestines, she held her hand over the wound for over six hours to keep them in place.

By around 5 a.m., sixteen more MARCOS had arrived at the Taj. This enhanced force now split into three teams. Two teams were deployed to evacuate injured civilians, the third searched for the terrorists. This third team reached the dining room of the Chambers, which had earlier served as the sanctuary for the civilians. The shiny cream-coloured granite corridor was brightly lit, but the room inside was dark. As the team entered the hall, there was deathly silence. Then they heard a soft but distinctive metallic rasp. It was the safety lever of an AK-47 being taken off. Gun flashes lit the dark hall. The terrorists inside the room fired at the commandos as they entered. One commando was hit as he ran for cover, a bullet entered his shoulder and another lodged itself in a spare AK-47 magazine tucked on his bulletproof vest. The MARCOS withdrew from the hall and evacuated their comrades.

The Taj staff informed the commandos that a large number of hotel guests were trapped in one of the four function rooms adjacent to the Chambers. The MARCOS chalked out a rescue plan as a dozen commandos closed in on the Chambers from two sides. Two MARCOS snipers, scaled the scaffolding around the Gateway of India, hefting Russian-made Dragunov sniper rifles. From here, they covered the large sea-facing windows that overlooked a basketball-court-sized open terrace, the roof of the hotel porch. Hotel staff told them these large windows were the only other access point to the Chambers. It seemed the terrorists had been cornered.

MARCOS tossed tear gas canisters into the Chambers and re-entered the hall, weapons at ready, at around 6 a.m. The terrorists were gone. Their escape route: a narrow staircase leading through the kitchen, back into the heritage wing of the Taj Palace.

In the Chambers dining hall, the commandos spotted a red rucksack left behind by the terrorists as they fled. It was brought down to the lobby, and the contents carefully opened and laid out on the floor. The Chinese-made rucksack belonged to Abu Umer alias Nazir, who had shot up the Leopold Café. The bag with 'Changing the tide' embroidered on it had a globally-sourced arsenal the commandos had seen in Kashmir: seven AK-47 magazines each with thirty 7.62×39 mm bullets. Over 100 loose M43 cartridges, to refill the magazines, a versatile AKM Type I bayonet which also functioned as an insulated wire cutter. An egg-shaped, blue Chinese Type 86P plastic-bodied fragmentation grenade packed with 1,600 steel balls with a six metre kill radius and a matchbox-sized twelve-volt battery, the kind favoured by militants to trigger off IEDs. The terrorists had clearly come prepared to inflict mass casualties.

But it was the four Arges 84 grenades that pointed the needle of suspicion across the border. The anti-personnel hand grenades were licence-produced by the Pakistan Ordnance Factory, Wah, from an Austrian firm Armaturen Gesellschaft mbH. Each half-kilo grenade had 5,000 steel balls packed around ninety-five grams of plastic explosives. When the pin was pulled and the grenade thrown, it exploded within three seconds. Each ball-bearing turned into a projectile with the velocity of a .22 calibre bullet, and could kill and injure within a twenty-metre radius. The Arges had surfaced in every major attack, with Pakistani fingerprints, the 12 March 1993 Mumbai serial blasts and the attempted storming of India's Parliament on 13 December 2001 by fidayeen attackers.

The rucksack also contained a small plastic pouch with black tangy tamarind pods used by soldiers on the subcontinent as a stimulant to stay awake. Another plastic pouch contained half a kilo of almonds and raisins, a high energy source carried by most fidayeen. It indicated one thing: Mumbai's attackers had come prepared for a long haul.

The commandos now turned to clearing the barricaded rooms. They knocked politely, explained they were from the armed forces, but never kept their fingers away from the trigger. They could not be sure if there were terrorists mingling with civilians. When Bhisham and Indra Mansukhani emerged from the Lavender Room at around 9 a.m., their eyes and nostrils were assaulted by the frozen tear gas smoke that hung outside. The corridor was a battlefield strewn with bullet empties and broken glass and shattered tiles. Grim-faced men in black asked them to raise their hands and walk out. Indra Mansukhani hesitated. She had lost her footwear in the stampede outside. The commando asked her to walk behind him, he cleared the glass pieces with his boots as he escorted them to safety. The Mangeshikars and the other guests walked to the safety of the hotel lobby helping out the wounded Rajan Kamble. (He later died in a city hospital).

The MARCOS' action was brief, but critical. They had saved nearly 200 hotel guests from certain slaughter. They had pushed the terrorists back into the Palace wing away from the Taj Tower, which they could have used for another siege. And if this was any consolation, the attackers had a depleted arsenal. It was a small victory in the dark hours of 27/11.

MARCOS at the Oberoi

The team of eight marine commandos deputed to Trident–Oberoi had less success. The eight-man team led by an officer and a dog squad with three Labradors reached the Trident around 2 a.m.

Commander Nagmote briefed them about the terrorist strike and how the two terrorists had swept into the Trident, killing everyone in their path. Nagmote explained the layout of the hotel and the three corridors that connected the twin hotels. The attention of the marine commandos was taken up by a bag lying near the reception counter. It was suspected to be full of explosives. The bag was inspected. It was a false alarm.

At 2.45 a.m., the commandos heard grenade blasts and firing from the poolside of the hotel. A team rushed to the third floor, and split into two. But by the time they reached, though, the terrorists had stopped firing and shifted their position. The commandos cleared the two levels up to the hotel poolside. Nagmote urged them to move in and tackle the terrorists. But they weren't taking any orders from him. The commandos stayed at the poolside, while the terrorists fired from the upper floors of the hotel. By 3 a.m., the twin hotel complex represented what was wrong with India's security apparatus: multiple agencies with different chains of command, no coordination or clear directives. There were naval commandos on the poolside, Central Reserve Police Force personnel, Mumbai police and troopers from an Indian army infantry arrayed on the Marine Drive promenade. All those assembled looked up at the looming towers of the hotel and waited for the NSG to show up.

The Den of Black Cats

Manesar / 10.30 p.m.

Col Sunil Sheoran was called a 'bullet catcher' in the Indian Army. That was the moniker for anyone who had survived firefights. Sheoran, it was said, used his body to trap bullets. 'If you are going into action, you don't need a bulletproof jacket – take Sheoran along.' Thus went the legend. It was a tribute to his resilience.

The thirty-eight-year-old commando had been shot twice. At close range. He had survived narrowly both times. A Naga insurgent had ambushed him from less than 5 metres away. An M-16 round fired at him entered his cheek and exited his neck just 2 mm away from the carotid artery. A 20-mm scar wrapped around his right cheek and under his ear. Then, in another firefight in 1996, an M-16 round had entered his chest just 5 mm above his heart. The bullet had gouged a matchbox-sized lump of flesh from his back as it exited.

Sheoran had taken over as group commander of the 51 Special Action Group (SAG) exactly two months ago.

The National Security Guards (NSG) – a centrally located SWAT (special weapons and tactics) team designed to overcome the deficiencies of local police units was raised by the Rajiv Gandhi government in 1985. Its motto was 'Sarvada Sarvottam Suraksha' (best protection always).

The 'Black Cats', as the NSG were dubbed for the black jaguar shoulder patches they wore, were modelled on Germany's GSG 9, created after the fiasco of the 1972 Munich Olympics. A botched rescue mission by German police led to the deaths of eleven Israeli athletes by Palestinian terrorists. In India, the May 1984 army assault on the Golden Temple eliminated Bhindranwale and his militant supporters but caused heavy collateral damage, an incident that indirectly led to the assassination of Prime Minister Indira Gandhi by her Sikh bodyguards. Mrs Gandhi's son and successor, Rajiv Gandhi, was quick to grasp the need for a central anti-terrorist force. NSG legend has it that Rajiv Gandhi personally selected their weapons and equipment.

Since the early 1990s, the NSG has provided close protection to VIPs on terrorist hit lists. These bodyguards came from the three Special Ranger Groups that drew its cadre from police and paramilitary forces. The NSG's offensive component, the Special Action Groups (SAG), comprised wholly of army personnel. 51 SAG specialized in hostage rescue and counterterrorist missions; 52 SAG in storming hijacked aircraft and sky marshal duties.

51 SAG vindicated themselves during the surgically precise June 1988 siege of the Golden Temple, dubbed Operation Black Thunder-II. Over forty militants of the Khalistan Commando Force were flushed out of the temple, with the unit suffering no loss.

On the night of 26/11, Col Sheoran, thick eyebrows furrowed, his piercing green eyes framed by rimless spectacles, peered at the shaky TV grabs showing spent cartridges after a shoot-out at Mumbai's Leopold Café. He recognized them as AK-47 empties. He had cleared the last files for the day and driven down to his bungalow in the NSG's 1,800-acre garrison in Manesar, in the barren Aravalli hills 30 km south-west of Delhi. This was no gang war, he said to himself; gangsters don't use AK-47s.

Sheoran had been alerted by a text message the Delta 8 unit, his makeshift arrangement where a commando in the complex monitored three television sets round the clock. Now as he watched the news, various scenarios began to unfold in his mind. At around 10 p.m., the news reported firing inside the Taj. 'A possible hostage situation.' Sheoran reached for his cellphone and dialled his second-in-command, Lt Col Sundeep Sen, who lived close by. 'Are you watching TV?'

At his home a few hundred metres away, Sen looked at the dead TV set at his home in Manesar. The Sens had snapped their satellite TV connection so that their son Divyaman, nine, could focus on his studies.

'Something has happened in Bombay,' Sheoran said. '*Kuch* militants *ghus gaye hain* hotel *mein* ...' he said.

'Militants?' Sen asked incredulously. 'Are you sure?' He went back into his bedroom, donned his uniform, picked up his rucksack and headed to the 51 SAG office half a kilometre away. As Sheoran's second-in-command, he knew what had to be done. If the SAG had to move, he had to work fast. Inside his office was a huge whiteboard, the duty chart of the 51 SAG, the location of all its officers and men. He sat behind his glass-topped table calling the unit officers and ensuring the force had adequate vehicles to move out of Manesar.

When Sheoran took over, there had been a few days of awkwardness. Sen was senior in service but Sheoran outranked him. Many officers opted out of this embarrassment of reporting to one's junior. But not Sen. He liked the NSG and was determined to complete his two-year tenure. In the new commanding officer (CO) he found a professional, unfussy about protocol. In just two months, the two officers had established an excellent working rapport. Tonight, Ram and Shyam, as they were jokingly called, had their task cut out. Sheoran was disappointed when he took over command of the

51 SAG. His army special forces unit in north-eastern India honed its combat edge against in surgents. In the 51 SAG, he saw a force living on past glory.

The commando unit had last seen action in the 24 September 2002 assault on Gandhinagar's Akshardham temple by a pair of LeT terrorists. The terrorists who massacred thirty devotees were killed by over 100 SAG commandos who had flown in from Delhi. Two SAG commandos had died in the predawn firefight with the LeT fidayeen. It took the Black Cats close to six hours to locate and kill the fidayeen inside the temple complex. But the NSG also sustained the first casualties in its eighteen-year history of over a hundred operations: Subedar Suresh Kumar, forty-two, part of a team looking for the terrorists, was shot and killed. Commando Surjan Singh Bhandari, twenty-six, who was shot in the head and seriously injured, died after two years in coma. India's largest-circulation English news magazine *India Today* called the attack on the temple 'Terrorism's new game plan'. Terrorists had now shifted to attacking soft targets. The immediate fallout of the operation was a pay hike from home minister, L.K. Advani: a 25 per cent commando allowance for the entire force.

Little attempt, however, was made to imbibe the lessons of Akshardham. Not that it was an easy task. The NSG's Special Action Group was a deputationist force; officers and men came from the army and then departed after their three-year tenure, taking their skills with them. A 1991 NSG proposal for a permanent cadre of 25 per cent specialist officers was ignored by the government.

Since 2002, it seemed, the SAG was in accelerated decline. Combat drills were not properly carried out. New equipment like ballistic shields had not been acquired, batteries for radio sets were constantly running out of charge, and the turnout of the men in the alert drills was shoddy. Training and standard operating procedures hadn't changed since the 1980s. The commandos did not have an urban cityscape with multi-storey buildings and staircases – they continued to train in a solitary 'kill hut', a rudimentary four-roomed brick structure.

Existing facilities like the sophisticated electronic firing range, with its array of moving targets in the sniper range lay broken and disused. The NSG went from being an elite commando force to the MHA's smallest paramilitary force. The SAG was a strange three-legged beast equipped by civilian bureaucrats, administered by the police and staffed by the army. Sheoran had to start from scratch. He decided to begin with core skills like training and alert drills. He often joined his commandos in cross-country runs and shooting to motivate them. He would place a 50 paise coin at the pistol-shooting range and encourage his men to hit it. His style was unhurried and non-formal; he called his juniors 'chhotey'. The alert drills were practised so often that a squadron commander's three-year-old son had begun saying 'A for Alert' in his playschool. Cynics in the unit joked that Sheoran could devote all his time to the unit because his family was away – his wife, Major Sween, was a military surgeon posted in Pune, his children were in boarding school.

Sheoran's second call was to Major Sanjay 'Kandy' Kandwal, the officer in charge of the 'alert squadron'. The 51 SAG had three squadrons with over 100 commandos in each. The 'squadron' was the Special Forces equivalent of an infantry company. In an emergency, the 'alert squadron' moved out of Manesar at a half-hour notice. This strike element formed part of the Counter Terrorism Task Force-1 (CTTF), a fully self-contained flyaway team of 150 NSG personnel which, apart from the 100-strong alert squadron, included a bomb disposal squad, a dog squad and a communications and surveillance team that could respond to a terrorist strike.

Sheoran received a call from Major B. Bharath, the third squadron commander on 'casual cycle'. 'Are we going to Mumbai?' Sheoran said only: 'luck baby, luck'. The NSG was alerted each time there was an internal security emergency, a bomb blast or a terrorist attack, but in the past few years, these had usually petered out. But the new CO had an inkling the bullets would follow him. 'Chhotey,' he told Bharath while practising a room entry drill in the kill hut, '*abhi main aagaya hoon* ...

kuch na kuch to hona hai ... tayyari kar le ... bahut jaldi hoga' (Now that I've come, there will be action ... very soon). By 10.30 p.m., even Sheoran was stumped at how prophetic his words were.

Mumbai was under unprecedented multiple terrorist attack. He was sure that it was only a matter of time before the NSG was called in. He decided to take his training officer, Major Sandeep Unnikrishnan, one of the 51 SAG's most important officers. 'Unni' was Sheoran's right-hand man because he put new army volunteers, officers and men, through their paces and assessed their worthiness for the 'Balidaan' (sacrifice) badge, the winged commando dagger.

At around 11 p.m., a two-minute hooter pierced the calm of the sprawling campus. It came from a siren-fitted van with flashing lights. The van drove around the unit lines, the rows of barracks where the commandos lived. The sound had an immediate response: a flurry of activity in the unit lines. Over 200 pairs of hands, roughened by years of firing and hard drills, sprang out of bed and instinctively reached for their black dungarees, boots and haversacks. The SAG was on the move. Every commando knew the drill. CTTF-1 had to be out of the gates of Manesar in thirty minutes. The haversack they called the 'alert bag' held twenty-five items essential for a seventy-two-hour deployment – a shaving kit; clothes: spare black dungarees, a pair of the army's combat dress, civilian clothes; food: a packet of instant noodles, roasted gram; and 500 rupees. It also held what passed off for the army's unofficial Meals Ready to Eat or MRE: shakarpara (deep-fried flour pieces coated with sugar). The men reached for their twenty-five-year-old GSG-9 'Romer' steel legacy helmets. Each weighed over 2.5 kg and was uncomfortable, equivalent to two bricks on your head, but protected the head from a 9 mm bullet and shrapnel. The troopers walked out towards their vehicles, briskly hefting their black helmets, bulletproof jackets and alert bags.

Commando Sunil Jodha, on guard duty at the lines, regarded the hooter with mixed emotions. He still had a month to go before his three-month NSG probation ended. 'Jodha ... *naye wale nahin jayenge*,' one of his comrades sniggered, as they filed past him. Jodha was distraught. He went to his bunk, picked up his rucksack, donned his black dungaree over his green combats and filed out with his comrades. If there was going to be action, Jodha would be part of it.

In another part of the complex, tube lights flickered on in the armoury called the 'koth' that lay deep inside the complex that held the NSG's arsenal. Rows of gleaming black Heckler and Koch MP5 sub-machine guns, Austrian Glock-17 pistols and the newly acquired grey Swiss-made SIG Sauer 551 assault rifles. Worn-out, three-foot-long synthetic boxes stacked inside held the

PSG-1 sniper rifles. Each weapon had a hand-painted numeral, meticulously entered into a register. The men started loading the weapons into trucks.

Another truck drove to the NSG's ammunition store, half a kilometre away. This truck loaded green wooden boxes containing three different types of ammunition. These boxes held matchbox-sized brown cardboard cartridges, stamped with the type of ammunition, from the Ordnance Factory Board's (OFB) Kirkee Ammunition Factory: 9×19 mm for the Glock, the MP5, 7.62×51 Marksman rounds for the sniper rifles, and 5.56 mm for the SIG.

Close to midnight, Sheoran received a call from Brigadier Sisodia, the man who was now in operational command. The brigadier directed Sheoran to take another team of fifty commandos from CTTF-2.

At 12.18 a.m., NSG headquarters flashed a code: 'Cheetah. Cheetah. Cheetah.' The NSG had been formally requisitioned. They had to move to Mumbai. This was not a training exercise. But the code was a formality. The 51 SAG was already on the move. Their men had begun forming up in the open ground near the unit lines; the equipment neatly spread out. Officers stood around engaged in light banter. There was Col B.S. Rathee, the deputy force commander, standing in for his boss, Brigadier Rangi. Lt Col Ramesh Kumar 'RK' Sharma, thirty-six, was slated to take over as the 51 SAG's second-in-command. An officer of the Gorkha Regiment, Sharma was a quiet man, but tough, and among a handful of officers over thirty-five to have cleared the NSG's probation, the gruelling firing and physical tests, under Unni's watch. And there was Major Kandwal, a tough Garhwali officer with a no-nonsense air about him. Kandy sported a beard, allowed only for Sikhs in the regular army. Special forces like the NSG, however, allowed their men a fair amount of leeway when it came to personal appearance.

Army officers deputed to the NSG came from infantry units, special forces, artillery, engineer and the armoured corps. The common thread binding them all was Major Unnikrishnan. Unni had been the 51 SAG's training officer for two years now. Lean and athletic, with piercing brown eyes and a booming voice, he epitomized an 'OG' or Olive Green officer, the army's informal nickname for by-the-book, diligent officers.

Unni had topped his commando course in Belgaum, earning a coveted instructor grading. He later served as adjutant – a post which administered discipline in the unit – for over two years at his parent regiment, the 7th Battalion of the Bihar Regiment. As training officer, Unni was merciless with officers and men who volunteered for the 51 SAG. Volunteers were put through a punishing six-week physical course called the probation where Unni was a laconic but formidable presence. At the gruelling obstacle course – a series of twenty-six ditches, rope climbs, rope slithering and wall scaling – he could be unsparing on stragglers: 'You are wasting the nation's time.' In the 'kill hut', a 3,000-square-foot set of six rooms and a shooting gallery where commandos learned crucial room-intervention drills, he emphasized speed and reflexes. 'When the bullet comes,' he growled, 'you won't have time to think.' At the sniper range, he went into details. Crouched beside trainees, he explained the precise finger pressure that would send a 7.62 mm bullet hurtling towards a cardboard 'Figure 11' target, a four-foot-tall charging infantry soldier, over 500 metres away.

Unni left his friendship at the gates of the training range, so friends could expect no leniency. But the tough exterior masked a gentle man. He worshipped his parents, Dhanalakshmi and K. Unnikrishnan, a retired ISRO employee settled in Bangalore. Unni was the man you turned to when a party had to be organized at short notice. He loved movies and drove late nights with his friends in the unit to the multiplex in Gurgaon's Ambience Mall, 22 km away, returning in time for three hours of sleep and morning PT at 5 a.m. He could drift off to sleep at a moment's notice. For the past year, he had wrestled with a divorce but never let that affect his work.

That night, Unni led the banter. Some TV channels had reported that over fifty terrorists had assaulted

Mumbai. 'Each of us should take two terrorists ...' Unni joked with his comrades Kandy, Bharath and RK. He turned to Captain Varun Dalal. 'Dalal, you rookie,' Unni said grimly, 'you get only one terrorist.'

Dalal grinned sheepishly. He had another month to complete his probation and was happy to be part of the operation. Dalal had been confined to his quarters after running high fever that morning, but the 11 p.m. hooter had chased it away. His body buzzed with adrenaline and anticipation. The young captain was in the company of men who had not the slightest doubt that they would prevail.

A hush descended on the gathering as Sheoran's white Gypsy King arrived. Bodies tensed, the men fell in line. Sheoran had held two open meetings with his troops here after taking over – army parlance called it 'feeling the command'. His talk was eerily prophetic then. 'Remember this,' the commando colonel told them, 'there is action wherever I go; you will all be blooded soon.' Tonight, he was to the point.

'Ready to leave?' was all he asked.

At 12.54 a.m., a motley convoy of nearly forty unmarked vehicles – transport buses, 4-tonne green-hued Stallion trucks and a small Swaraj Mazda pickup truck – swung out of the gates of the Manesar garrison. Major Kandwal's white Maruti Gypsy King shot ahead of the convoy and the trundling mass of trucks entering the capital city.

The SAG was an interventionist force, not a guard force. This meant it would inherit a crisis – usually a hostage situation. To intervene, the force had to arrive at the scene fast, and for this, it needed a dedicated transport aircraft. But to get to the aircraft parked at Delhi's Indira Gandhi International Airport, the commandos had to move 30 km by road. During 'Operation Vajra Shakti' in 2002, the NSG convoy spent an embarrassing two hours negotiating peak-hour traffic on National Highway 8 between Manesar and Delhi. The force arrived in Gandhinagar at 10 p.m., five hours after the terrorists struck.

Little, it seemed, had changed since then. If anything, the traffic situation had worsened. NH-8, between Delhi and Jaipur, had come to be the country's busiest intercity route, used by a quarter of a million vehicles each day. There were two toll barriers between Manesar and the airport. Kandwal and his men got off their vehicles and had a brief scuffle with the toll-booth staff who refused to keep the gates open for the convoy that was following. 'Don't you understand … this is a national emergency,' he snarled at them. Two toll gates opened for the SAG.

Fifty-five minutes later, the SAG was within sight of New Delhi's Indira Gandhi International Airport. A new gigantic airport terminal and a third runway were being built. The area was a floodlit construction site with giant gantry cranes, and echoed with the rumble of drills and concrete mixers. But the convoy skirted this and headed towards an unmarked gate at the south-western corner of the airport, kicking up a cloud of dust as it crossed the rutted construction sites.

The khaki-clad Defence Service Corps sentries at the gates were the only indication that this was a government installation. Brown, six-foot-high gates slid open to reveal a giant blue hangar and a large compound lined with trees and landscaped gardens. It was an oasis of greenery and calm amidst the chaos outside. The area was not marked on any map. Neither did the secret air force unit comprising Soviet-built Ilyushin 76s, Boeing 707s, Antonov 32 transports and sleek Gulfstream jets appear on any official aviation list. And for a very important reason. These aircraft were the covert eyes, ears and wings of India's external intelligence agency, the R&AW.

The convoy was met at the gates by Major Arun Jasrotia, who led the SAG's sniper detachment. Jasrotia, a quiet, sharp-faced second-generation army officer, had been decorated earlier with a Sena Medal for gallantry in the Kashmir Valley. For the past fortnight he had been on deputation with the 52 SAG based near the airport. He flew each day as a sky marshal. Dressed in plainclothes, he mingled among the passengers on sensitive domestic sectors, keeping a wary eye for potential hijackers. Tonight, he would fly on another mission.

The trucks drove up to a single Ilyushin 76 standing at the taxiway of the tarmac. The giant four-engine-plane was a silhouette. Only its cargo hold was open and lit, its ramp lowered on the tarmac. Since the inception of the NSG nearly a quarter of a century ago, one IL-76 always remained on round the clock alert, to fly the commandos to a counterterrorist emergency anywhere within the country. The aircraft had been topped up with 70 tonnes of fuel and was ready to take off. Air force crew in their distinctive blue overalls walked around and conducted last-minute checks.

The SAG knew the drill. The troopers manually loaded nearly twenty tonnes of equipment off the trucks and into the aircraft. To the bystander this might have looked chaotic; it was anything but. This SOP (special operating procedure) had been in practice for decades. Each squadron knew the sequence and where and how it had to load its equipment. Manifests were ticked off and the cargo stacked in the centre of the aircraft. It took them half an hour to load up. The Indian Air Force (IAF) loadmaster on board covered the cargo with canvas netting. It was 2 a.m. The IL-76 was ready for take-off. The pilots walked around to the NSG personnel asking them to hurry up; they had to take off soon. But the NSG were waiting for a very important passenger.

Shortly before 3 a.m., Home Minister Shivraj Patil drove up to the aircraft in his white ambassador car. He was dressed in a black achkan, salt-and-pepper hair immaculately greased back. The minister, escorted by NSG's Director General Jyoti Krishan Dutt, strode briskly up towards the waiting cargo jet. He walked up the steep crew ladder on the side and boarded the aircraft. For a cabinet minister who whizzed around the country in an Embraer 'Legacy' 135 BJ business jet operated by the Border Security Force, the IL-76 was more than a little short on conveniences. But tonight, his spartan ride would convey a very important message.

No politician bore the brunt of the ongoing wave of bomb attacks in India more than India's internal security minister. The seventy-three-year-old politician from Maharashtra's south-eastern district of Latur had suffered an embarrassing defeat in the 2004 Lok Sabha elections. It was only a momentary hiccup. Patil swiftly landed the second most important job in the United Progressive Alliance cabinet, chiefly due to his unquestioned loyalty to the Gandhi family.

On 13 September 2008, when five bombs had killed thirty people in Delhi and injured over a hundred, the media savagely attacked Patil. The home minister had found time for three wardrobe changes between 7.30 and 10.30 p.m. 'He hits the wardrobe as Delhi burns,' screamed the headlines of the tabloid *Mail Today*. The NSG operated under Patil's ministry. But Patil hadn't come to wave goodbye or display sartorial solidarity. He would accompany his troops to Mumbai. It would show the people and his cabinet colleagues that he was very much in charge.

Patil paused momentarily and looked at the NSG personnel inside the cargo hold. With a brief smile and a wave of his hand, he acknowledged them. He then ducked and headed forward into the extended crew compartment behind the pilots.

It was 3 a.m. when the wheels of the IL-76 retracted and the aircraft swung southwards towards Mumbai. The IAF called the Soviet-built aircraft the 'Gajraj' or king of elephants. Tonight, its interiors were packed like a crowded Mumbai passenger cattle car. A dull light illuminated the aircraft's off-yellow interiors. The centre of the cargo hold was occupied by rows of metal boxes, suitcases and crates was secured by nets. These contained over 200 assault rifles and sub-machine guns, 40,000 rounds of ammunition, 20 kg of plastic explosive and over 150 hand grenades. Weapons and ammunition were stored separately to prevent accidents in-flight.

The IL-76 also had a modular upper deck, a retrofit that could be pushed in to comfortably seat 225 fully equipped soldiers. But it was missing in this aircraft, so the 200-strong task force sat in rows on the canvas and aluminium seats and rested their heads on the panels along the sidewalls. A dozen commandos sat on top of their cargo. Some stretched themselves on the load and slept. Walking down the aisle was an arduous task, involving stepping over toes while balancing yourself against the load.

The seven-member aircraft crew was busy at their flight stations. Dutt, Sisodia and Patil occupied the passenger seats that had been placed in the extended crew compartment, which usually housed two beds to rest extra pilots during long-range missions. Patil was contemplative and quiet for the duration of the flight. Dutt, meanwhile, laid out the broad brushstrokes of the operation to Brigadier Sisodia: there would be minimum collateral damage, the safety of the hostages was paramount and the terrorists would have to be taken alive as far as possible. He was supremely confident the operation would go off well. 'What do we call the operation?' Dutt asked at the top of his voice. Sisodia thought for a few minutes. 'Well, there has always been a tradition of calling them Black ... so, Black Tornado?' he suggested. Dutt gave it the thumbs up.

In the cargo hold, Sheoran briefed his squadron commanders. They sat bunched inside just behind the crew compartment. Unni, Kandy and Sharma strained and leaned forward to listen to his voice above the high-pitched roar of the aircraft's four turbofans. Intelligence about the assault was scarce. In the air, they operated in an information vacuum. So Sheoran focused on what he could do: get his commandos into the scene of action as soon as he could. He split the SAG into two teams.

Col Rathee would lead operations at the Oberoi with Lt Col R.K. Sharma. Sheoran would be in charge of the Taj operation where Majors Kandwal and Unnikrishnan would lead commandos. 'We have to hit Mumbai fast and do our duty,' he said. 'We are better trained than the terrorists, so let's just remember our drills.' He got his officers to synchronize their watches. They gave a thumbs-up sign.

'*Arrey* Brat Sir,' Unni drawled to Major Bharath sitting next to him. '*Dekhna, jab tak hum pahunchenge, sab khatam ho gaya hoga, hume kuch karne ko hi nahin milega. Aur* sir, *aap zyada bak-bak mat karna, main soney jaa raha hoon* (By the time we get there, things will be over. And please don't chatter, I'm going to nap now).' With that, he turned to one side and slept.

As the aircraft approached Mumbai, Sheoran took the aircraft's public address system and pep-talked his troops. '*Bahadur sheron,*' he said, '*tumhare imtihaan ki ghadi aagayee hain.*' He then sat down and furiously scribbled a set of tactical questions he would ask the Mumbai police: the description of the terrorists, what they were armed with, where the hostages were and whether the terrorists had opened negotiations with the government. Yet there was a sense of unease at the back of Sheoran's mind. The Black Cats were going into the city blind. Most officers and men had only heard of the two landmark Mumbai hotels they were supposed to operate in. A few had even seen it from the outside during personal visits to Mumbai. The terrorists had already familiarized themselves with the layouts before they left Karachi. Now they also had a six-hour head start over the NSG.

Assault on the Taj

27 November, 9 a.m.

Deputy Commissioner of Police (DCP) Nisar Tamboli squinted at his watch. It was 5 a.m. The grey IL-76 aircraft taxied down to a remote bay of the air cargo complex at Mumbai's Chhatrapati Shivaji International Airport. Tamboli, a slim, soft-spoken officer with deep-set eyes and a high forehead, was part of the reception party. Six hours earlier, the deputy commissioner of police (Zone VIII) had received a call from Rakesh Maria, the joint commissioner of police (Crime), coordinating operations from the police control room. Maria's instructions were concise: escort the NSG from the airport to the city. At that time, Tamboli was examining a two-foot-deep bomb crater at Vile Parle. The bomb had been planted in a taxi. Pieces of the driver's body had landed on trees and buildings several hundred metres away.

Tamboli had no idea how many commandos to expect but when he saw the full complement inside the aircraft, he was glad he had arranged for twenty single-

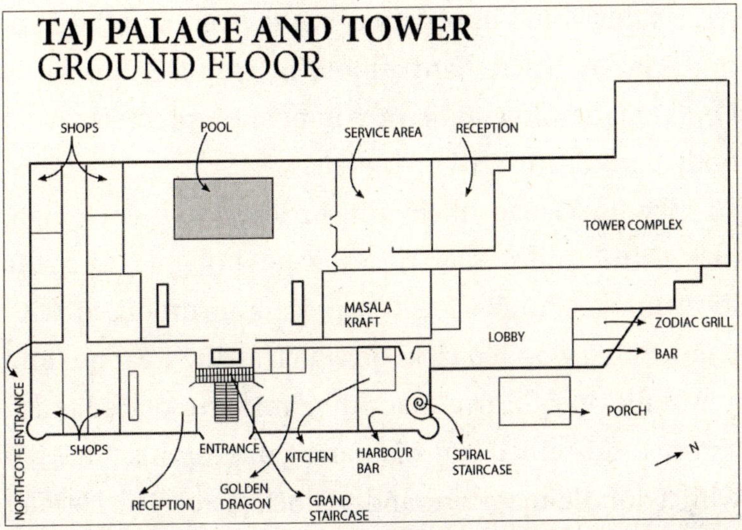

decker BEST buses. Home Minister Patil alighted first. He was escorted to a white Ambassador car that would take him to Mumbai's Raj Bhavan, the residence of the state governor.

The team commanders Sisodia, Sheoran, Rathee and Kandwal drove down to the police headquarters. Captain Dalal and Major Jasrotia were escorted to a police van. They were welcomed by a kindly Mumbai police driver in khakhi, who jabbered in Marathi through the hour-long drive. The two officers could only nod politely – it was a language neither of them knew.

Their force, meanwhile, kitted themselves out on the concrete runway apron. Each commando carried over 15 kg of gear. The heaviest item was an 8-kg bulletproof jacket made of Kevlar. The jacket had two hard armour panels that fitted into sleeves in the front and the back of the jacket. These hard armour insert plates known as HAPs, made of ceramic or composites, protected vital body parts against AK-47 bullets.

They unloaded their hit boxes – two-foot-high, black tin trunks. The boxes were bought from the local market for Rs 1,200 a piece and modified with handcrafted wooden racks on which all the weapons and ammunition of a five-man hit team were placed. Each commando pulled out his personal weapons: an MP5 with a double-magazine and a Glock pistol. The Heckler and Koch MP5, or Maschinenpistole was compact, just 21 inches long, simple to use, accurate and unjammable. Ever since the German firm introduced it in the mid-1960s, most special forces worldwide favoured this weapon. It fired 9x19 mm low-velocity rounds held in a thin, curved, thirty-round detachable box magazine. The 9×19 mm was the ideal cartridge. Unlike the high-velocity AK-47 rounds, it did not ricochet in confined spaces. The NSG had three versions of the MP5: regular, silenced and compact. The commandos inserted four spare magazines for the MP5 and the Glock into their bandoliers and stocked up on stun grenades and HE 36 fragmentation grenades.

Last to go in was the distinctive balaclava and the black Romer steel helmets. The SAG had 250 of these German-made helmets, just enough to equip half the force. They resembled motorcycle helmets, had been imported over two decades ago and looked their age. The headgear was constantly refurbished through Indian 'jugaad' like chinstraps from motorcycle helmets and coats of cheap black paint over the original dull matte finish.

In full battle gear, the commandos began the orderly march towards a fleet of red BEST buses and police vans. The buses were marked 'SP' for Special and had 'Reserved' written on the side in Marathi. Over 200 pairs of boots scrunched up the aluminium floors of these vehicles, with the commandos gingerly moving their guns and equipment boxes through the narrow doors meant for one passenger to board or alight. It took them another twenty minutes to load the buses.

As the NSG convoy wound its way to the city, the troopers looked at the handful of people that had ventured out on the roads, fear and puzzlement writ large on their faces.

At around 5.30 a.m., Brigadier Sisodia, Col Rathee and Col Sheoran were ushered into the Mumbai police control room in Crawford Market. The control room had a large electronic GIS (geographic information system) map of the city that showed the location of police stations and various police vehicles. Over twenty-five policemen sat in two semicircular rows before the map, manning the twelve police zones in the city. Maria moved from one police operator to the next, each one of them speaking non-stop. The police had suffered an unprecedented casualties, so he regarded the arrival of the NSG with some relief. Maria was yet to interrogate the sole attacker, Ajmal Kasab, whom Assistant Sub-inspector of Police Tukaram Omble had heroically captured.

He walked around to the pulpit-like elevated table, where the control room officer sat, gesturing the officers to sit before him. The action had since moved to the Taj and Oberoi hotels, he informed them. There were four terrorists inside the Taj. Maria furnished a physical description based on eyewitness accounts. Most of the terrorists appeared to be in their late teens or early twenties. One of the terrorists was tall, well built and wore a red cap and T-shirt, he said. The marine commandos, the police and anti-terrorist squad had laid a cordon around the site. The NSG would get a detailed briefing on the hotel layouts from the staff there.

Worried that media reportage could compromise the operations, Brigadier Sisodia asked Maria, 'Can you do something about the media? I believe they have been reporting our arrival.'

Maria shrugged. He couldn't do anything about the media, but promised to keep them at a safe distance so that they wouldn't interfere with the operations.

The fifteen-minute meeting with Maria gave the NSG a fix on numbers, but little else.

Sheoran, meanwhile, scrounged for tactical intelligence. From the police headquarters, his vehicle sped to the state police headquarters near Regal cinema. He met the director general of police, Anami Roy. The meeting was brief and uneventful. The DGP could not add to what Maria had already told them. Sheoran pocketed the list of queries he had scribbled in the IL-76 and headed back to his vehicle. Arriving at the Taj hotel, he alighted from the front door of the white Qualis under the magnificent rectangular porch. It was crowded with police and fire department vehicles. He heard a distinct tak-tak sound echoing through the upper floors – MP5 on single-shot mode. The sound pleased him. If a firefight was on, it meant security forces were in contact. If so, his men could close in and swiftly neutralize the terrorists. Sheoran strode into the lobby of the Taj and was struck by the distinct smell of tear gas mixed with cordite. It was the smell of urban combat. Sheoran was back in the front lines, only this was in the heart of the city.

'Sir, we have a hostage situation at the Chambers.' A young marine commando officer had walked up to the colonel to hurriedly brief him.

Sheoran's commandos arrived a few minutes later. He led his officers to the pavement outside the Taj. He laid out a few twigs to explain the layout. The palace section of the Taj was U-shaped; its two wings – north and south – enclosed the swimming pool. A patio linked the old wing to the tower block to the north. 'Kandy, get your hits to work,' he said. The colonel also radioed Unni – who had reached the state secretariat with the main body of the NSG commandos and was waiting for orders – to reach the Taj swiftly. Unni and Kandy's teams would sandwich the terrorists at the Chambers.

As a marine commando escorted Kandy up to the Chambers, his nose wrinkled at the smell of tear gas. The MARCOS were lobbing tear gas grenades into the rooms around the Chambers with textbook precision. 'You will run out of grenades pretty soon,' he said to them, coughing.

Kandy quickly summed up the situation. The MARCOS had been guarding the guests at the Chambers and had prevented a slaughter. But they had broken contact with the terrorists several hours ago. They could not spare manpower to pursue the attackers down the corridors.

'Sierra One, this is Sierra Five. No hostiles in contact,' Kandy radioed.

Sheoran grimaced. The terrorists had slipped away. His force was primarily geared towards hostage rescue within confined spaces. They stormed rooms only after terrorists had been corralled in. While hostage negotiators bought time, the Black Cats planned the rescue.

He did the math. The Taj Palace and Tower had 1,100 rooms. They were like two separate hotels. Occupancy was reported at 80 per cent. There were close to 3,000 guests when the terrorists struck twelve hours ago. Four terrorists were on the rampage. He had just forty commandos to clear all the rooms and fight terrorists. This operation could take days. He would not ask the MARCOS to operate with him. The two commando units had different drills. In a firefight, this could have two unhappy consequences – crossfire and fratricide.

At 9.30 a.m., the NSG commandos became the third force to take over operations at the landmark hotel. It had been only twelve hours since the terrorists had struck.

Sheoran's immediate priority was clear: evacuate 'technical hostages', civilians trapped in the operation zone. The commandos would then close in on the terrorists. The fires of the previous night had knocked out the CCTV cameras in the Palace wing. Sheoran now needed eyes on the target, at least on the outside.

'Jassi, Jassi,' he called for his sniper chief. Major Jasrotia appeared hurriedly. 'You're my eyes, get to work,' Sheoran said.

Jasrotia knew what he had to do. He walked off briskly to look for vantage points to position his snipers.

In Operation Black Thunder – the seventy-hour siege to evict militants from the Golden Temple – in 1988, NSG snipers were atop numerous buildings around the shrine. They acted as spotters and sentries: militants who strayed out of the complex were shot. The NSG had two months to prepare for Black Thunder.

Sheoran inspected the contents of the haversack recovered from the terrorists after the firefight at the Chambers. It was neatly laid out on the floor of the lobby. The grenades and AK-47 ammunition were an eye-opener. 'Our friends from across the border,' Sheoran thought to himself.

Just then, Unni walked in with his task force from the state secretariat. The lobby of the Taj was packed. Police, paramilitary forces, fire brigade and rescue staff milled about before a thirty-foot-long magnificent M.F. Hussain canvas triptych – horses, lions, doves and a peacock called 'three stanzas of the new millennium'. Sheoran looked for a secluded spot to brief his men. He spotted a room to the left of the lobby, past a Louis Vuitton display window. This was the Harbour Bar, India's first official watering hole. The '1933' beneath its signage denoted its vintage and, in more sedate circumstances, helpful barmen told you its liquor licence number was '001'. It looked out onto the Gateway of India and offered a splendid lateral view of the ships and yachts at anchorage. The cyan walls of the nautical-themed bar were lined with white wooden panelling. It had circular Burma teak tables and an antique brass telescope, ship sextants and copper-hued vintage diving helmets. The bar had a ten-foot-long, wood-lined, black granite bar counter. The wine shelves behind brimmed with hundreds of bottles of the city's finest Merlots and limited-edition single malts, covered with delicate velvet.

At the bar, Sheoran swiftly divided his force into two teams – Kandy would head Task Force Tower, Unni would lead Task Force Palace. Sheoran carried two walkie-talkies, one for each task force. A third handset kept him in touch with his snipers.

'Your priority will be hostage rescue,' he told Unni. 'We can sort out the terrorists once we take out the civilians.' As Sheoran turned to leave the bar, he noticed a majestic copper-hued spiral staircase. It led up towards the ceiling and was tucked away in a corner of the bar, behind a stone arch. 'And, Unni, find out where this leads to … we can use it …' he said before striding out to a makeshift command centre in the lobby.

Major Jasrotia walked around the massive Taj hotel complex. The fire brigade used the lull in fighting to evacuate guests from the Taj Palace. Tall fire ladders and a hydraulic lift extricated frightened civilians out of the hotel rooms through the windows. One of the civilians, a well-dressed lady on the second floor, matter-of-factly passed her handbag to a fireman and then gingerly climbed over the window onto the fire lift.

Jasrotia saw the Gateway of India as an obvious sniper perch. The monument was undergoing a facelift and was covered with iron scaffolding, which made it easier to climb. Marine commando snipers had begun climbing down. They would now be replaced by Jasrotia's men.

The 400-foot-long hotel promenade that overlooked the harbour posed a problem. There were no buildings for snipers to sit on. Jasrotia then walked around the Taj. The gate at the rear was locked and chained. He climbed a tree to look over into the compound. Bodies of guests were scattered near the poolside. He held his hand out to see if anybody fired. There was silence. He then turned to look above. Crowds had gathered on the roofs of a row of buildings behind the Taj intrigued by the sight of a commando in helmet and bulletproof vest, scaling a tree. They craned their necks over parapets for a closer look. Jasrotia waved them away using both his hands.

At 9.10 a.m., Jasrotia's snipers moved to the rooftops of five buildings behind the Taj. One sniper team under Captain Varun Dalal climbed atop the Gateway of India while Captain Dalal and his buddy, Havildar Mustafa Pathan, went up the top floor of the 162-year-old Royal Bombay Yacht Club. They carried with them two German-built PSG-1 sniper rifles. These rifles were heavier than the Dragunov sniper rifles that the army and Marcos used. The PSG was deadly accurate upto 300 metres. In the hands of a trained sniper, it had a 99.9 per cent chance of hitting its target with a single shot.

From the roof of the six-storey Devidas Mansion, a residential building overlooking the Taj Palace and Tower, Jasrotia lifted his walkie-talkie and spoke. 'Sierra One, this is Sierra Six. Snipers one, two and three in position.'

In the lobby of the Taj, Sierra One, Sheoran, cocked his head sideways and spoke into the walkie-talkie clipped to his collar. 'Sierra Six, this is Sierra One. I read you. Over.'

The SAG guns ringed the hotel, covering all exits from the hotel in deadly interlocking fields of fire. Now the Black Cats could move into the hotel.

Task Force Palace

Task Force Palace under Major Sandeep Unnikrishnan moved in to scan the 268 suites in the Palace wing. This did not include the numerous restaurants, ballrooms and banquet halls. In the lobby, Unnikrishnan – in tan-coloured running shoes with thick rubber soles, ideal for a building intervention – lowered his mask and briefed his hit teams in chaste Hindi. 'Our main objective is to rescue the civilians,' he told them, eyes sweeping his team. 'Do not touch anything in the rooms without asking me.' Unni was concerned that terrorists might have booby-trapped the hotel to slow down the NSG. 'One careless move by you can kill your comrades.'

His men slid the safeties off their MP5's fire selector switch above the trigger and switched it to single-shot mode. They were trained to fire only accurate single shots. Sunlight streamed into the magnificent building. The corridors smelt of smoke. The teams did not have maps, but they couldn't afford to wait.

After ninety tense minutes, Unnikrishnan's teams had scanned all the rooms on the ground and top floors of the north wing. They cleared the Wasabi restaurant and rescued ten persons hiding inside. No sign of the terrorists. But there were telltale marks of their presence. Corpses lay where they had been shot. Pools of blood coagulated around them on the opulent granite floors. The commandos did not touch the bodies. Militants frequently booby-trapped dead soldiers in Jammu and Kashmir and in the north-east of India. All it took was a grenade minus its pin, its lever held in place by the weight of the corpse.

At around 1 p.m., the twenty-member commando team moved their search-and-rescue operation to the southern wing, MP5s cocked, fingers on triggers.

Major Unnikrishnan planned to clear the rooms from top down. Two hit teams led by Naib Subedar Fire Chand Nagar and Naib Subedar Karpe clambered up to the rooftop of the palace wing. They scanned the roof for terrorists hidden among the rows of water tanks and equipment. When the men reached the sea-facing suites on the sixth floor, they were greeted by a deathly silence. The fires of the previous night had been doused. A Taj employee deftly wielded a master key to open doors. Most suites were bolted from inside. The men in black knocked on the doors. 'We are NSG commandos. We are here to help. Open the door.' They knew they were giving themselves away to potential terrorists. But they had no option. No one knew who was in the rooms. It was a chance they had to take.

By 2 p.m., twenty-three frightened guests had been escorted down to the lobby. Two hours later, the number of rescued guests swelled to forty. But where were the militants, Nagar thought to himself. Could they have escaped in the melee of the previous night?

At 6 p.m., Unni's men reached Room 402 on the fourth floor. They knocked. There was no response. They introduced themselves in Hindi. Then in English. Silence. The hit team waited for a few minutes. Then, Fire Chand braced himself against the wall and kicked the door open. Shots rang out from inside the room. The bullets flew past the door. One passed through Nagar's left foot, shredding his black jungle boot. A splinter hit Commando Sunil Kumar Yadav. A ferocious gun battle erupted. The NSG had finally made contact.

Yadav closed in on the room under cover fire from Havildar Rajbir Singh, who also approached the door stealthily and lobbed a grenade inside. It exploded. A fire spread through the room. The terrorists started closing towards the door where Yadav had taken up position.

Major Unnikrishnan was informed about this contact. 'Take cover, take cover, I'm coming,' his voice crackled over the radio. He dashed with five troopers to the place of contact. He reached the spot and evacuated the injured Fire Chand and Commando Yadav to the Operations Control Centre (henceforth Op Centre) on the ground floor of the Taj totel. The terrorists had fled. They left a burning room and dead hostage behind. It was quarter past seven.

At around 8.15 p.m., Major Unnikrishnan returned to the Op Centre to brief Sheoran. Smoke had filled the fourth floor; his men could not enter it to clear rooms. They had to think of an alternative route. The weary members of TF-Palace walked to a corner of the Op Centre for food. The menu was frugal, the standard military fare of aloo-puris. The hotel kitchens were shut because there was no water or electricity. The food came from the local military unit, packed in cardboard boxes. As he sat on the sofa to eat, Unnikrishnan noticed that his buddy Sunil Jodha looked unwell. 'Sunil,' he asked, 'why are you sweating?'

'Sahab, I'm wearing dungarees over my combats ...' Jodha replied sheepishly.

'Take it off', Unni ordered.

Jodha looked around the lobby. There were dozens of hotel guests, police and army personnel.

'Okay, go ahead, I'll cover you.' Unni moved on the sofa. Jodha sat on the floor, unzipped his dungaree and quickly extracted his green army uniform from beneath. No sooner had he done this than Unni was gone.

Task Force Tower

Major Kandwal and his four hit teams moved up the fire escape of the twenty-one-storeyed Taj Tower. They were trained to work their way down a building, but Kandwal reversed the drill. If there were terrorists in the Tower, they could spill out into the lobby for another attack. His commandos would work their way up the hotel. They would have to assume there was a terrorist behind every door. But with seventeen rooms on each of the twenty-one floors, it would be a tedious exercise.

In 2002, Kandwal had sneaked into a twin-storey brick house in Kashmir disguised as a local. He lugged a 10-kg IED under his phiran. Two hard-core militants had been reported to be in the empty house. Kandwal's IED blew out the roof and collapsed the walls. The two militants were crushed to death. In the Taj, their priority was to rescue hostages.

Kandwal had a red master card in his pocket. It could open any door in the hotel, but not if the door had been bolted from the inside – like most doors were that day. The commandos had to use their persuasive abilities. 'Open up please, we are here to help.' They

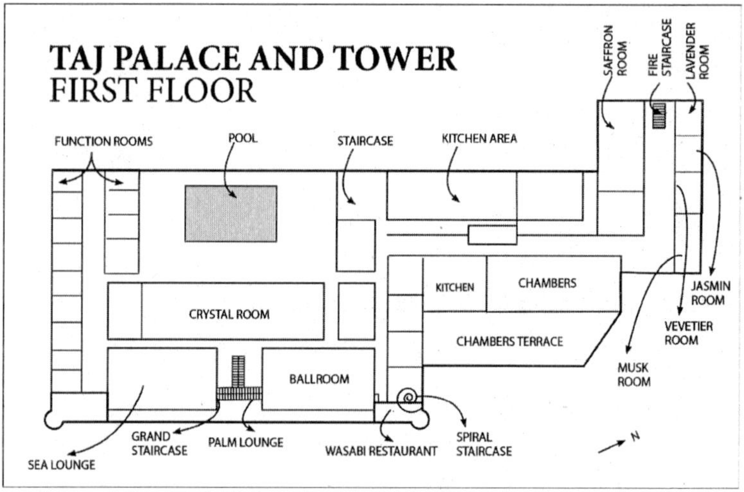

had practised room entry to perfection in the 'kill hut', where five commandos stacked up literally one behind the other. Here too, they rapidly entered one after the other, covering the corners with their guns. They checked under the beds and behind the curtains. Two hit teams of ten commandos searched the rooms. Two more teams guarded the stairwells.

Each L-shaped floor had seventeen rooms. But after clearing a few rooms, it was evident the task would be arduous. Each door opened into an antechamber that led into the room. The space was only ten feet long and three feet wide. It would be tactically unwise to crowd five men in. Kandwal changed the drill. Now on, only a two-man buddy pair would enter. Five buddy pairs would alternately clear rooms to avoid exhaustion.

BHASKAR PAUL

The boat ramp at Machhimar Nagar where the ten terrorists landed

NSG

Sunil Kudiyadi, security chief at hotel Taj Mahal Palace and Tower, briefs the commandos on the location of the terrorists

NSG

Home Minister Shivraj Patil enters the IL-76 aircraft carrying the 51 SAG commandos

NSG

The gloomy interior of the IL-76. Colonel Rathee is seen sitting on the cargo

NSG

Colonel Sunil Sheoran briefs his team commanders inside the IL-76 as NSG-DG JK Dutt watches. (L to R) Major Kandwal, Major B Bharath, Lt Col R.K. Sharma and Major Jasrotia

NSG

NSG Commandos enter the lobby of the Taj

NSG

Hotel guests rescued from their rooms in the Taj lobby

NSG

Commandos reloading MP5s in the lobby

NSG

The grand staircase leading to the Taj ballroom with the bust of J.N. Tata where Major Unnikrishnan and his men were shot at

NSG

An NSG commando at the spot where the terrorist who shot Major Unnikrishnan had positioned himself

NSG

The Palm Lounge where Major Unnikrishnan was killed in a firefight with terrorists

NSG

The Harbor Bar and the Wasabi restaurant on fire with the terorrists still inside

NSG

Commandos outside the Harbor Bar
where the terrorists made their last stand

NSG

The sniper's perch on
a fire brigade sky-lift
outside the Taj

NSG

Guests being rescued from the hotel while terrorists fire from inside the Harbor Bar

NSG

A satphone and AK-47 recovered from one of the terrorists

NSG

NSG personnel check bodies of murdered Taj kitchen staff for explosives

NSG

Ratan Tata, Chairman of the Tata Group, examines a 9 mm bullet case while R.K. Krishna Kumar speaks with Major General Abhay Gupta in the Taj lobby

NSG

The driveway through which the terrorists entered hotel Trident

NSG

The lobby of the Trident where the terrorists struck killing guests and counter staff

NSG

The Kandahar restaurant in the Oberoi where terrorists massacred diners

NSG

The view up the polygonal atrium of the Oberoi

NSG

The fire-damaged Room 1856 where the terrorists made their last stand

NSG

The view down into the atrium

BHASKAR PAUL

Side view of the lane showing Merchant House and Nariman House

NSG

TV cameras cover the NSG helidropping commandos on Nariman House

Helidropped NSG commandos walk down into Nariman House

Lt Col Sundeep Sen and commandos fire at the terrorists inside Nariman House

Abu Umer, the second terrorist killed at Nariman House

NSG

The Holtzbergs' living quarters on the 4th floor of Nariman House where the terrorists made their last stand

NSG

Pistols and AK-47s recovered from the two terrorists. Havildar Gajender Singh Bisht's MP-5 is seen on the right

The abandoned rooms were snapshots of life rudely interrupted by the terror attack – unmade beds, stale food from room service the previous night on the table, digital cameras plugged into laptops and the steady trickle of baths overflowing. The guests who were trapped inside whispered to their relatives on phones, the fearful ones hid in their closets and under beds. One US-based NRI businessman, had been furiously chanting the Hanuman Chalisa when he was rescued.

'Sierra Six to Sierra One. Movement on floor ten. Window. Friendly. Over,' Jasrotia radioed Sheoran.

Jasrotia and his sniper teams watched all the guests who stood at the windows or walked about in their rooms. The CO relayed the message to Kandwal.

Rescued guests were gathered in a safe room on each floor. Once an entire floor had been searched and cleared, Kandwal deputed one hit team of five commandos to escort the guests downstairs to the Op Centre. By 6 p.m., forty-six guests had been brought down this way. A dozen more floors remained. The commandos had been awake for nearly two days. They had shed their alert bags with its food supplies in the IL-76. These were to have been brought back later by the Mumbai police, but no one knew where the bags were. So, the commandos scooped up the mineral water bottles, soft drink cans and dry fruits they found in the rooms into laundry bags. That would be their only food for more than a day.

As the commandos cleared the hotel spaces, a critical deficiency now came to light: they did not have the manpower to guard the rooms they had cleared. A second planeload of commandos sent from Delhi was yet to arrive. Sheoran tried to fill the breach with a dozen CRPF commandos. The policemen would act as 'stops' or barriers in the Chambers and the first floor. They would cut off the terrorists' escape downstairs. But Sheoran was too optimistic. A few hours later, he heard shots. The CRPF commandos had rushed back down into the lobby because they had heard movements there, and had fired. Sheoran sighed and pushed his five-man hit team to man the first floor to replace them. He waited for reinforcements to fly in from Delhi with Lt Col Sundeep Sen.

Around 8 p.m., reinforcement strickled in. Captain Anil Jakhar and twenty commandos moved up to the Taj Tower to assist Kandwal's room clearance. Kandy was edgy. The stream of requests from NSG brass to evacuate certain guests on priority was beginning to play on his nerves.

Meanwhile, his search parties pounded up the stairs to the twelfth floor of the Taj Tower. Tension ran high. At 11 p.m., a frantic message came from the ATS. Phone calls were being made from a room on that floor to Saudi Arabia. The commandos rushed to room 1201. There were muffled sounds of movement inside. The NSG commandos placed a shaped charge, a piece of plastic explosive on the lock, and blew the door open.

There were four guests huddled in the room, two Saudi nationals and two Indians. 'Take off your clothes,' Kandwal shouted, pointing his MP5 at them. The four complied and stripped to their undergarments. They were civilians.

'Room 1201 clear. Friendlies,' Kandy radioed back.

At around 11.45 p.m., Joint CP Deven Bharti received a call from police control room about a woman trapped in the Taj. Bharti was the NSG's liaison man in the Taj. He wore a khakhi-coloured flak jacket over a cream-coloured half-sleeve shirt and dark blue trousers. The call to Bharti had taken a convoluted route. Priya Florence Martis, who had hidden herself in the data centre of the Taj Palace ever since the shooting began on the night of the 26th, had also phoned her uncle who in turn informed police control room. Another colleague, Manish, was hiding in another part of the server room. They had not had any food or water since the terrorists had struck.

Bharti walked up to the reception with Brigadier Sisodia. He dialled the extension to Florence's office. A frightened voice whispered at the other end. Bharti put the call on speakerphone so that Sisodia could hear her. 'Ma'am,' the Brigadier asked her, 'where are you?'

Priya was confused, she barely knew her way around the hotel. All she could mumble was, 'On the second floor …'

'Don't worry, my commandos will come and get you,' Sisodia reassured her. He scribbled her location on a piece of hotel stationery and passed it on to Sheoran.

Sheoran directed Major Unnikrishnan to evacuate her. The NSG officers worked out an alternative route to reach her – through the grand staircase areas of the heritage wing. Unni quickly drew up a plan to approach the second floor through the staircase. These were among the last areas yet to be cleared. DCP Nangre-Patil's men had taken heavy fire from the militants at this staircase the previous night. Unni didn't know this.

Death of a Hero

At 1 a.m., on 28 November, Major Sandeep led his hit team, Sunil Jodha, Manoj Kumar, Babu Lal and Kishor Kumar through the pièce de résistance of the Taj: the grand staircase – a single, long staircase split into two like a Y. At the landing between the two arms, sat a garlanded bronze bust of Jamsedji Nusserwanji Tata, founder of the Tata business empire and the man who built the Taj in 1903. Tata wore a phenta, the traditional Parsi black cap, and stared sternly into the distance. Behind the bust was a large entrance to the Palm Lounge that had long since been boarded up and covered by a huge mirror.

The staircase was pitch-dark. The fire brigade had poured thousands of litres of water at the fires in the Taj. The water now seeped down the floors and dripped into the cavernous staircase area. The sound of dripping water added to the eeriness of the place. It was like entering a smoky jungle cave. A thick red carpet with floral patterns was fastened to the steps by thick brass stair rods. The carpet was soggy and oozed water, which meant that the commandos' boots made a gentle squishing sound as they walked up the stairs towards the bust.

As the hit team walked up the stairs, gun flashes lit up the darkened stairway. The terrorists were firing at them from above. Unni signalled Sunil and Babu Lal, to head up left and towards the heavy brown doors that led to the Palm Lounge and the ballroom. They were to throw grenades and clear the Palm Lounge. The two commandos walked up gently, weapons drawn. They took positions on either side of the doorway. The doors were shut.

Just then, a grenade flew out of the darkness. It bounced on the carpeted staircase and exploded. An AK-47 rattled from above. Bullets drilled the staircase. They punched into the walls around the doorway, digging into the stone and plaster. The glass around Tata's bust shattered. It was an ambush. The terrorists were on high ground. They had seen the silhouettes of the NSG men. And they had waited. The atrium was now a kill zone. Major Unnikrishnan moved under the cover fire provided by his two commandos.

Another grenade sailed out from one of the top floors and exploded on the granite floor. Over 5,000 ball bearings from the grenade blasted a deadly pattern around the staircase. Sunil Jodha's body was riddled with bullets and splinters. He collapsed and rolled back down the stairs to the foot of the bust. The commandos took cover and blasted away at their unseen enemy. Blood oozed around Sunil's body. Two bullets had entered his chest. One had been trapped by the ceramic rifle plate on his bulletproof jacket. His left arm was lacerated with steel ball bearings. 'I'm going to lose my arm,' he thought to himself as he lay prone on the floor.

Unni rushed back to Sunil. He saw blood streaming out of his buddy's wounds. 'Take him back for first aid,' he hissed at Babu Lal. In a flash he had gone back up towards the Palm Lounge, alone.

Unni swung up his MP5 and fired a burst across the atrium. The bullets hammered into the wall. Then he bounded up the stairs leading to the other set of doors opening into the Palm Lounge. It was a terribly risky move because he didn't have a buddy to cover him. If he broke contact, the cat-and-mouse game would start all over again. He decided to outflank the terrorists. His running shoes made no sound. He could see the outlines of the large wicker chairs and tables strewn before him.

He felt his bandolier. He only had a white flash-bang grenade left. He flicked the pin off the grenade and flung it into the lounge. The grenade exploded with a loud crack that rattled the windows. Unni dashed in. He then fired a burst at the sea-facing windows. Clear! He looked around the wall. A brown ornate grille in front of him covered the ballroom like metal foliage. The ballroom was his target. He held his MP5 in front of him as he swiftly charged down the corridor. To his left was a small alcove with two sofas and a circular granite tabletop. There was a flash from beneath the table and two near-simultaneous sounds – the rattle of AK-47 and the burst of an MP5.

'Sierra Five, Sierra Five ... this is Sierra One, come in. Over.'

Col Sheoran's message pulsed aimlessly through the airwaves around the Taj. There was no response. 'Perhaps he is in close contact, he won't speak ...' Brigadier Sisodia said. The NSG rapidly cleared the charred southern end of the hotel, the Sea Lounge on the second floor. NSG commandos now guarded all the vital access routes into the northern end of the hotel.

By 3 a.m. on Friday, 28 November, Major Kandwal's weary team had cleared all twenty-one floors of the Taj Tower. Kandwal handed the Tower back to the Mumbai police. Four hours later, all the rooms in both hotels were cleared of potential hostages. Now the hunt for the terrorists would begin. But where was Major Unnikrishnan?

Sheoran climbed up to the fourth floor and peered down the grand staircase into the atrium below. Bodies, limp and contorted, still dotted the galleries around the atrium. 'Saabji, look at the bodies,' one of his commandos, Havildar Digh Ram, whispered. The bodies were bloating. It had been over thirty-six hours since the terrorists had struck. The air was thick, foul and nauseating. It smelt of putrefying bodies and rotting food. The bodies could not be removed till the NSG did their 'Render Safe Procedure' to clear booby traps. For that to begin, the buildings had to be cleared of terrorists.

Sheoran, however, was searching for Unni. He looked closely at the first floor where they had made contact with the terrorists. It had four doors. One of those doors, diagonally opposite the bust, was open. The door led into the hotel. Perhaps, Unni had gone looking for the terrorists in the opposite direction.

At 6.30 a.m. Jasrotia's radio on the roof of the residential building crackled urgently. 'Sierra Six, this is Sierra One, come to Op Centre. Over.' Sheoran needed more hands to augment the search for the missing major. The size of the teams was reduced. Jasrotia was given two hit teams and tasked to move and search the first floor.

He would start from the kitchen area where Major John, a newly inducted officer, had taken position.

Sheoran's officers repeatedly dialled Unni's mobile phone. It was switched off. If Unni was in the hotel, he was being very quiet.

At around 9.30 a.m., Major Kandwal and Major Jasrotia retraced Unni's steps. They advanced as a two-man buddy pair. Jasrotia aimed his MP5 in front. Kandwal, covering the rear, aimed his MP5 above him. A black figure lay prone on the marble floor, face up. Unni! His left leg was folded under his right. His right arm lay outstretched, left arm across his chest. His body was riddled with bullets and lay in a sticky black pool of blood. All the bullets had been fired from the left. The fatal round had pierced his head from the lower jaw and exited the skull. His walkie-talkie lay two feet away from his head. It was neatly placed on the floor, upright, switched off. The ring of a flash-bang grenade pin hung around his thumb.

It didn't take long to figure out what happened. The terrorist had been hiding in the alcove behind the statue, crouched under the table and two sofas. He had shot the lone Black Cat as he charged down the corridor. Unni had taken a burst from an AK-47. His body had twisted around as it hit the floor. The terrorist had taken his weapons and retreated northwards into the hotel. But the officer had not gone down without a fight. He had instinctively fired at his assailant. Bullets from Unni's MP5 were embedded on the wall and the wooden lattice. A bloodied running shoe of a terrorist lay nearby. A trail of blood led towards the ballroom. Unni had wounded the terrorist.

Kandwal reached for his mobile phone and not his walkie-talkie. No one could know that an officer was down. 'Sir, Unni no more. Confirmed.' There was a brief pause. Col Sheoran's voice did not betray his anguish, 'OK. Wait. I'll send someone.'

Major Sandeep Unnikrishnan became the NSG's first officer to die in combat. His death shook the 51 SAG. It was the death of a beloved colleague and a reckoning of their own mortality.

Unni's death slowed the operation at the Taj. The NSG brass reassessed their moves. They became cautious. They would not waste any more lives. His death was, however, kept away from the troops. Sheoran did not want it to affect their morale.

Major Unnikrishnan's last charge pushed the terrorists towards the restaurants at the northern end of the Taj Palace. They could run no further. Sheoran was determined not to let Unni's death go in vain. He moved his snipers to cover the north wing. Sheoran called down Captain Dalal and his shooters from their perch atop the Yacht Club.

Dalal instinctively knew something was wrong. He felt a cloud over the command centre at the Taj but asked no questions. The CO had orders for him. Dalal was to take his two-man sniper team into a fire brigade sky lift. The Mumbai Fire Brigade's 'telescoping articulated platform', was critical in rescuing hostages from the upper floors of the Taj. Now it would be used as a sniper perch. The platform was positioned on the road just 25 metres away from the northern corner of the hotel. Dalal and Mustafa Pathan clambered onboard. The six-square-foot cage had just enough place for three persons including the operator who manoeuvred the platform. The snipers took their bulletproof vests off and placed it in front of them to create an improvised shield. Sheoran directed Dalal to ensure the terrorists would not target the media, which had been moved to the far corner of the Gateway of India. The PSG-1 gun barrel now aimed at the Taj Palace, wary eyes peered through its rubber-lined Hensoldt-scope, looking for the terrorists.

Next, Sheoran directed his teams to move into the ballroom.

The commandos tiptoed in. It was pitch-dark. They warily tore down the thick drapes that covered the windows and began searching the room. It took them nearly five hours to complete the search. The ballroom was clean.

Meanwhile, Priya Florence Martis, trapped in the data centre, whispered over the phone to friends and family. She had been terrified by the sight of a figure in black moving into her room. She saw a gun barrel. The intruder, she couldn't quite tell who, appeared to be looking for something. He paced around the room and then went away. She huddled in her hideaway, tired, hungry and thirsty. There were a dozen bottles of water at a table in sight. But she was too terrified to venture out. 'Get up and drink, get up and drink,' a friend repeatedly egged her on the phone. She bit her lip and resisted the urge to move out.

The figure was Col Sheoran. He went back down to the hotel lobby and dialled her number. Priya answered the phone.

Sheoran said he would come and get her. But he had to first ensure she was not in trouble. 'Ma'am, are you a hostage?' he asked her several times. She replied in the negative. 'When you come to my room, please call my name, else I won't come out,' she said.

Sheoran briskly walked back towards the data centre on the second floor. The door was open. There was no sign of anybody inside. He looked around and spoke,' Florence, Florence, we have come to save you …'

A voice emerged from below. It was weak. 'I'm here …'

Priya Florence had lain in a foetal position under a tiny table for thirty-six hours. She could barely walk. Sheoran helped her up. But the girl refused to leave. 'Please save Manish ... I won't leave without him,' she insisted.

Manish, a colleague in her department, had hidden in the server room after bullets smashed a glass door. Sheoran went in search of him. He carefully scanned the room but found no one among the bank of servers. He even looked up at the rafters. Nothing.

'There's no one in the room,' he told her.

'Are you sure?' Priya was insistent.

Sheoran went back to the room. His patience was wearing thin. Then he detected a movement in the floor. The floorboard moved. Sheoran gently lifted the panel. He was surprised by what he saw. Manish had wedged himself under the floorboards in an area used to conceal wires. The space was less than a foot deep. Tired and exhausted and in deep shock, the executive had to be hauled out and helped to his feet by two commandos.

An hour later, Florence, Manish and five tourists rescued from their rooms had been escorted to safety downstairs. The hotel was now clear of all civilians. All three radio sets crackled. Three hit teams now encircled the restaurant and plugged all routes into it.

At around 11 a.m., Mustafa spotted a movement in the Wasabi restaurant. A hand emerged from behind the curtains of the restaurant. It was holding a grenade. Dalal squeezed the trigger of his weapon. A bullet crashed against the thick glass. The hand dropped the grenade, which fell on a black car parked below and exploded, showering ball bearings upwards.

'Sniper Four to Sierra One. Cannot see through curtains. Militants have advantage,' Dalal radioed Sheoran.

Director General Dutt of the NSG, who had been reviewing the operations at the Oberoi, now drove to the Taj. He had heard of the death of the officer. A pall of gloom hung over the Op Centre in the lobby. 'Take me to the location,' Dutt said, wanting to see first-hand what had happened. If the NSG's operation was flawed, he would review it. 'Sir, it's too risky,' warned Brigadier Sisodia. The NSG was still in contact with the terrorists. But Dutt was insistent. Sisodia asked for a few minutes and walked away. Dutt heard the intensity of firing from his commandos increase. Sisodia had evidently ensured that the terrorists kept their head down.

Dutt was ushered to the grand staircase. The NSG officers explained the situation to him. The terrorists were cornered in the north wing. Now, it was only a matter of neutralizing them.

'There is nothing wrong in what we are doing,' Dutt told the NSG bosses triumphantly. 'The operations will continue.' The statement lifted morale.

Shortly before noon that day, Dutt received an unusual visitor. Unusual, because the operations were on in full swing. It was Lieutenant General Noble Thamburaj, general officer commanding-in-chief of the army's Pune-based Southern Army Command. The commander was in combat fatigues. He sported a 9 mm Browning army issue pistol on his waist. He had flown into Mumbai accompanied by his personal staff and his wife Anita Thamburaj. If someone noticed the impropriety of an army commander touring a building with his wife while operations were under way, they did not mention it. Thamburaj was the seniormost army officer south of the Tropic of Cancer. He was briefed about the operations in the lobby of the Taj by Deven Bharti and Col Sheoran. 'Finish it quickly,' Thamburaj said before striding out of the Taj. It was an overstatement. Sheoran already knew what had to be done.

Outside the Taj, the army commander briefed the waiting media. The new wing of the Taj had been sanitized and handed over to the police, he said. One terrorist, possibly two, had moved into the adjacent old heritage building. 'It is just a matter of a few hours before we wrap up things,' he said.

At 4 p.m., Kandwal, Jasrotia and Jakhar led their hit teams into the north wing. The lack of ambient light slowed them down. They moved deliberately as they combed the rooms that led to the Wasabi. Reaching the doors to the Wasabi kitchen, the officers positioned their men at all four entry points into the restaurant.

They stood in the stewarding area before two doors that led into the restaurant. The doors were made of tinted glass with thick wooden frames. It was dark inside the restaurant – the commandos could see themselves reflected in the glass. They heard faint noises. Whoever was inside was on the move and was certainly not a civilian.

Their eyes fell on a six-foot-high refrigerator that stood on the side. It was the Wasabi's 'hot cupboard' where the restaurant stored dishes before they were served at the correct room temperature. Kandwal and Jasrotia hefted it to barricade the door on the right.

'Sniper Four, take a single shot,' Jasrotia radioed Dalal. A bullet crashed through the window and slammed into the cupboard. Dalal could provide them with covering fire.

The commandos crept up to the door and placed a wooden frame against it. The frame was wrapped in gunny sacking. It was packed with a kilogram of plastic explosive Kirkee, named after its ordnance factory of origin. The commandos trailed a wire from the door frame and joined it to a 12-volt battery. The thick wooden doors exploded inwards. Crack! Crack! Two AK-47 bullets came in through the doors.

Kandwal swore and picked up his carbine and squeezed the trigger. Bang! Bang! Bang! Three toe-sized 9 mm brass empties tinkled on the marble floors.

'How many are there inside?' he thought to himself. 'How many?'

The terrorist inside was a disciplined shooter. He shot off one or two rounds to conserve ammunition.

'Cover me, I'm going inside,' Kandwal gestured to Jasrotia.

Two more bullets flew out of the restaurant. It hit the other side of the door. Sparks ricocheted off the stone masonry. Jasrotia grabbed Kandwal. 'Sir,' he pointed at the bullet marks, 'there's more than one terrorist inside.' The terrorists had taken positions at opposite ends of the room. The only entrance into the Wasabi was now a funnel of death.

The AK-47 fire continued. Grenades rolled down the floor and exploded. The commandos fired back and rolled grenades inside. They exploded but had no effect on the terrorists. The gun battle continued for another forty-five minutes.

The noise of the fight was deafening. Bullets clanged into the kitchen utensils. The air was thick with the smell of cordite. The commandos scrunched brass empties with their boots as they raced to change position.

Col Sheoran followed the progress of the battle on his radio sets. He took off his spectacles and gently wiped the sweat off them onto his uniform. His mind was racing and his scarred, stubbled face was a picture of focus. Both terrorists at the Oberoi had been killed. The fight at Nariman House was ending. He had to terminate operations at the Taj without risking further casualties. It was pointless sending men in – the terrorists did not hold hostages.

The four terrorists could not have chosen a better place for their last stand. The Taj Mahal Palace was like a medieval fort with two-foot thick stone walls. The north wing bulged like a semicircular battlement with windows overlooking the road. The Wasabi and the Harbour Bar nestled in the safety of its stone walls. The grenades being tossed inside seemed to have no effect.

Sheoran fell back on his unit's only heavy weapon, a Carl Gustav 'rocket launcher' or RL that fired milk bottle–sized high-explosive shells. A few well-aimed shots from the RL would vaporize the terrorists and end the siege, he reasoned. But Dutt and Sisodia overruled him. The blast wave could damage the structure. Besides, Dutt reasoned, with the media watching, they could not use heavy weapons against the Taj.

So Sheoran went back to the task of knocking down the windows so that his commandos were covered as they advanced into the bar and restaurant. 'Sniper Four, can you destroy window?' Sheoran radioed Dalal. The sniper team fired four shots in quick succession. The bullets crashed into the glass, creating neat holes. But the laminated safety glass was at least 10 cm thick and shatter-proof. The PSG's rounds only ventilated it. Dalal swore silently.

'Sniper Four to Sierra One. Cannot break glass. Over,' Dalal radioed back.

Sheoran called in the automatic grenade launcher (AGL) he had borrowed from the local army unit. The tripod-mounted launcher spat out 30 mm anti-personnel grenades. Each potato-sized grenade could kill personnel within nine metres of it. Sheoran used it as a sledgehammer to destroy the windows.

The first round flew out of the AGL and bounced onto the road, well short of the target. A misfire. The fuse inside the grenade was activated only after the projectile had flown 75 metres. A soldier ran across, casually scooped up the round and walked across the road to fling it into the sea. Sheoran then took the weapon a little distance away and aimed it. The AGL fired seven more rounds with deadly accuracy; it made a sound like a military drum roll. Four windows were shattered, the frame and green curtains hanging limp.

Dalal reported movement inside. Two grenades sailed out onto the road from two sides of the restaurant and exploded on the road outside. A volley of single-shot AK-47 rounds was fired towards the sniper and the hotel lobby.

At 6 p.m., the fire brigade lit up the restaurant area using halogen lamps.

The battle for the bar and restaurant raged on. The NSG grenades and bullets proved ineffective.

Kandwal radioed Sheoran. They needed IEDs and not grenades. Col Mann, an engineer officer with the NSG, bound two HE 36 grenades with a small slab of plastic explosive. It would triple the effectiveness of the grenades, he promised. The explosives were wrapped together with black duct tape. Mann grinned as he noted that the tape had 'ISI', for the Bureau of Indian Standards, stamped on it. His men made a dozen such grenades and handed them over to the commandos.

Sheoran, meanwhile, moved his hit team onto the seafront road outside to prevent the terrorists from fleeing. Another hit team under Captain Ryan Chakravarty of the NSG's anti-hijack squad, moved to the central lobby of the first floor to cut off the terrorists' exit.

At 11.30 p.m., Dalal fired a few rounds to pin down the enemy. The commandos lobbed in their improvised grenades into the bar and the restaurant through the kitchen and from the ground floor. The explosions were terrifying. The windows of the bar and the restaurant exploded and showered the road with glass. Snipers fired into the Wasabi. At 2 a.m. on 29 November, small fires began licking through the restaurant. Jasrotia and his commandos attempted to enter but were stopped by heavy fire from inside.

The Black Cats started hurling hand grenades and tear gas shells to cover the entry of Captain Anil Jakhar's hit team of five commandos. But the terrorists advanced towards the door, firing bursts of AK-47. The exchange of fire continued. At the cartridge-refilling centre in the lobby, troopers opened brown cartons of 9 mm bullets and refilled MP5 magazines. The magazines were carried up to the commandos.

Kandwal tried a forced entry from the second door. Gunfire opened up from multiple directions. There were at least three terrorists inside.

The NSG's bullets, even the improvised grenades, seemed to have no effect. The terrorists were entrenched behind the heavy furniture. Two of them were sheltered behind the thick pillars of the restaurant and the wooden serving counters they moved in to form makeshift defences.

One terrorist used the spiral staircase to alternately fire from between the roof of the Harbour Bar and the floor of the Wasabi. The stair rungs protected him from grenade splinters; the stone arch from bullets fired by the NSG commandos.

The gun battle continued. It was hazardous to walk the granite corridors of the north wing. A thin carpet of empty cartridge cases covered the floors. At 6 a.m., the fight turned into a fire. The liquor in the Harbour

Bar ignited. The terrorists started moving downstairs to break out of the windows.

From the road adjacent to the restaurant, Sheoran hurled several hand grenades inside the Wasabi. Fire engulfed the restaurant and heavy smoke billowed out of the windows. One of the terrorists screamed from inside, '*Rabba reham kar!* (God, have mercy)'.

Major Kandwal, Major Jasrotia, Captain Jakhar and Naik Sate Singh leapt out of the kitchen and onto the terrace above the porch. They started firing onto the windows of the restaurant. Tongues of flame and a thick column of smoke leapt out of the windows. Two terrorists headed for the window. Kandwal saw them coming. His MP5 blazed at them for a few seconds. They fell down backwards. Another terrorist in the Harbour Bar tried to escape through the southernmost window of the bar. He was shot thrice by Major Roy from the bar door. He fell onto the pavement outside. It was Shoaib, one of the Leopold Café gunmen. Varun Dalal saw one more terrorist sitting next to the window and covering Shoaib's exit. He fired once. The body slumped down.

Shoaib's smoking body lay on the pavement just below the bar. Sheoran dragged the still burning corpse away and dumped it in the centre of the road.

By 7 a.m., the north wing of the Taj was engulfed in smoke. Fire brigade tenders poured water into the restaurant and bar. An hour later, the commandos entered the burnt shell of the restaurant that was now in ankle-deep water. Burnt bodies of two more terrorists were recovered from the foot of the staircase. The body of the fourth terrorist was however missing. A frantic search began. Kandwal poked under part of a false ceiling that had collapsed near the window of the harbour bar. He extracted a burnt AK-47, its stock still folded. Beneath the weapon was the burnt torso of Abu Umar alias Nazir, fossilized and unrecognizable. All four terrorists had now been accounted for. The siege of the Taj had ended.

The operations, however, would continue until nightfall. Commandos, dog squads and engineers swept both hotels for explosives. Sheoran and his men stayed awake. That evening, they had their first formal meal at the Hotel President in Cuffe Parade. There, most commandos slumped down on the tables and passed out. They had to be carried away. After more than three continuous days of operations their bodies had pronounced 'mission accomplished' and switched off.

Action at the Oberoi

On the night of 26/11 Deepak Bagla, forty-six, was late for dinner. The delay cost him his reserved table with the seaside view at the Kandahar. But it also saved his life. New Delhi–based director of the British international private equity firm 3i, Bagla was dressed in blue jeans, a white half-sleeved T-shirt and monk shoes. He wanted to unwind, after a day of hectic business meetings, with a leisurely dinner. Bagla and Michael Queen, his London-based chief executive, had to settle for a table near the kitchen. After a repast of grilled fish, butter chicken and nan, they were waiting for the bill when they heard what they thought were firecrackers. Then the crackle grew louder and seemed like it was walking into the restaurant. Three minutes later, there were screams from inside the Kandahar. Bullets flew around the room, hitting diners sitting by the seaside windows and shattering the glass. 'Michael!' Bagla shouted, 'Run!' The duo shot past the kitchen doors and arrived at a winding fire escape leading to the lobby. They instinctively decided to go up to Bagla's sea-facing room 1269, just two floors above the Kandahar.

The firing continued. Grenade blasts reverberated like mini-earthquakes through the atrium. Bagla spent a few minutes creating a bunker in the room. He took a chair and wedged it against the door, then filled the basins in the bathroom with water and instructed his colleague not to use the flush because the noise could give them away. They crouched on the floor near the bed and waited for help.

Task Force Oberoi

At 9 a.m. on 27 November, a white Mumbai police jeep with Col B.S. Rathee, Lt Col Sharma and Major B. Bharath barrelled down the road that led from Mantralaya towards the Oberoi–Trident. The three infantry officers inside were a mixture of youth and experience: the deputy force commander, Col Rathee, portly and bespectacled, close to retirement; Lt Col R.K. Sharma, who was just days away from getting his commando badge; and Major Bharath, one of the NSG's most experienced officers. Bharath, five feet seven inches tall, lean and in peak physical fitness had been in the NSG since 2006, first as training officer and later as squadron commander of the NSG's third squadron. He had switched places with Major Unnikrishnan six months ago.

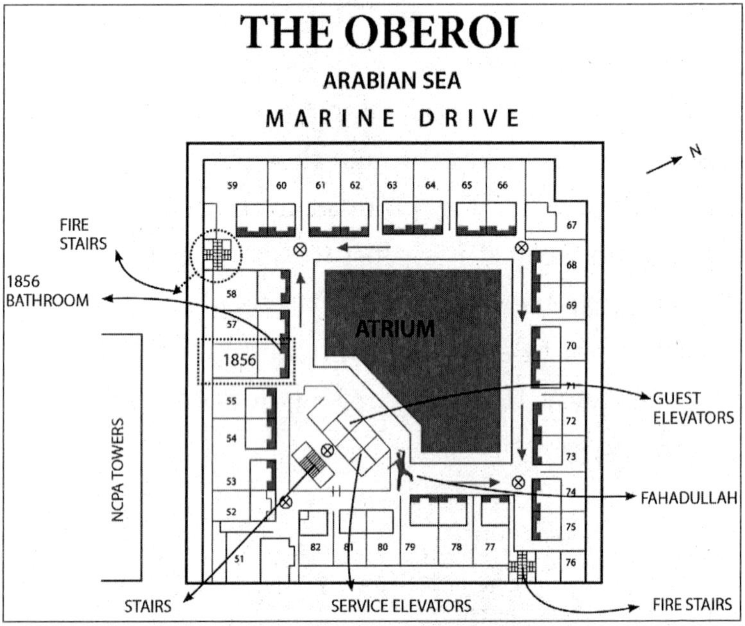

The three Task Force Oberoi officers were mentally processing the information they had just received from the police at the Taj. A plan had begun to take shape. Terrorists at the Oberoi had taken hostages. They had to be swiftly neutralized and guests rescued. It sounded deceptively simple. Their troopers had assembled at the Mantralaya, the only secure government building in the vicinity.

The jeep turned left and halted in front of the Air India building. This was where the police had set up camp and where Police Commissioner Hasan Gafoor's official vehicle was parked. The police had tied a yellow plastic rope across the Marine Drive to block traffic. Behind this flimsy barrier stood the surging media line and the rows of tripod-mounted cameras. TV cameras captured the three NSG officers getting a situation report from the police. It would be their only glimpse of the Task Force Oberoi. Additional Commissioner of Police (South Region) K. Venkatesham had moved the media lines back to nearly half a kilometre away from the Oberoi.

Venkatesham now briefed the NSG officers. The terrorists holed up in the Oberoi had targeted the police and marine commandos with AK-47 fire and hand grenades, he said. They had shot guests and taken some of them as hostages. They didn't seem to be in the Trident, the officer told them, they were somewhere in the Oberoi. 'This is the Trident ...' Venkatesham said pointing at the buildings, 'and that is the Oberoi ... the rest, you know what to do.'

Major Bharath looked up at the massive hotel complex in some frustration. This intelligence was insufficient to plan an operation. Then came an unexpected breakthrough. A six-foot-tall young man in jeans and a yellow checked shirt walked up to Bharath and introduced himself. He was Captain Anurag Grover, an officer from the 21st regiment of the Parachute Regiment's Special Forces. The twenty-seven-year-old captain was on long leave, just days away from getting his formal discharge from the army. He was doing a business management course in Mumbai and had boarded a local train and rushed to the spot when he had heard of the attack the previous night. He wanted to ensure his friend, Captain Bhupendra Dhamankar, a retired Special Forces officer on duty at the hotel, was safe. He was. The young captain was one of the three assistant security officers who worked under Nagmote. Tonight, he was glued to four CCTV screens in the security room in the basement of the hotel. On the bank of screens, Dhamankar and Grover played back the noiseless but horrific footage: attackers walking into the Trident armed with AK-47s, mowing down hotel guests and staff in their path, as they headed down a long corridor lined with showrooms that led into the Oberoi. The footage ended there. There were no CCTV cameras in the Oberoi.

There were two terrorists, Grover told Bharath, and they had headed into the Oberoi. 'They are upstairs, somewhere on the nineteenth floor,' he said. 'They are dropping grenades into the atrium,' he said. Grover then whipped his phone out and showed the grim screen shots of Fahadullah and Abdul Rehman walking across the lobby, assault rifles in hand. This precise input helped the NSG in two ways: it told them what their enemy looked like and confirmed that they were indeed in the Oberoi. Now, the commandos could focus their attention on the smaller hotel. The commandos would attempt a stealthy entry into the hotel. Sharma instructed the hotel authorities to disconnect the cable

TV connections. He did not want the terrorists to know the NSG had arrived.

Bharat sought a quick word with Col Rathee. 'Sir,' he requested the deputy force commander, 'the terrorist will die either today or tomorrow, but don't rush me into the operation. Let me do it calmly. I want to carry back all these forty-nine boys.'

Col Rathee knew the request came from one of the 51 SAG's most experienced officers. 'Do the operation the way you want to do it,' he said. For the next forty-two hours, the colonel was a benign presence, letting his two officers conduct the operations.

Meanwhile, Nagmote, the hotel's chief security officer, had sent his deputy to meet the NSG with the hotel blueprints. Rajesh Kadam, twenty-eight years old, an athletic six-footer, Elphinstone College's star striker in Bombay University volleyball matches, wore a black shirt, khakhi-coloured cargo pants and brown leather shoes as he crossed the road and headed for the roadside where the police brass had assembled. He was one of the hotel's three assistant chief security officers who worked in eight-hour shifts. He also doubled up as a fire safety officer, which continued the family tradition: his father was a fireman posted in the Colaba fire station and would have been dousing fires at the Taj had he not been away at the family village in Sindhudurg District, that week. Kadam, who lived with his parents in the Colaba market area, rushed back to work after a frantic call from his boss, Commander Nagmote. He met the security chief in the lobby of the hotel and heard the gunfire. He thought it was a liquor-fuelled brawl, but only for a moment. Kadam knew the sound of firearms. He had fired .303s and SLRs in his five years of NCC training in school and college. The AK-47s and grenade blasts told him something was terribly wrong.

The two unarmed hotel staffers had attempted to help the security forces breach the Oberoi the previous night. At around 2 a.m., Nagmote escorted eight marine commandos upto the pool level of the Trident. Kadam directed a dozen Anti-Terrorist Squad personnel up the fire escape at the Oberoi towards the other swimming pool on the same level. The terrorists hurled grenades and fired at the ATS personnel from above, the sounds of the blasts amplified by the atrium. The ATS and the MARCOS were forced to give up their rescue attempt.

Rajesh then did the next best thing. He escorted the shaken hotel guests to an assembly point the management had created at a nearby shopping mall. Now, nearly twelve hours after the mayhem had begun, he was composed as he walked up to the commandos and introduced himself. The commandos, however, had no time to sit and understand the detailed, carefully rolled up drawings that Rajesh brought with him. The operations had to begin immediately.

'Get us to the rooftop,' Sharma said bluntly. So, the young officer explained the access points to the roof. The Trident had three umbilical connections with the Oberoi: at the lobby level, at the pool level, and a route that not many knew – from the basement two floors below the ground. The terrorists had used the lobby-level stairs to enter the Oberoi and had also gone to the poolside. The fire escape that began on the pool level, Rajesh told them, was the only safe route to go upstairs.

The ten-storeyed Oberoi hotel was the group's flagship luxury brand in Mumbai. It stood sandwiched between the Trident and the NCPA Towers, both of which were twenty-one storeys tall. The Oberoi's floor count began from the 'tenth' floor on the pool level, so the hotel's twenty-first floor was really only its tenth floor. Like most hotels, it didn't have a thirteenth floor.

As Rajesh accompanied the fifty commandos, Sharma realized he was indispensable. 'It's a complex environment,' Sharma told Rajesh as they walked down towards the basement. 'If it's OK, we want you to accompany us.' He could not force Rajesh to put his life on the line.

Rajesh gave him a look of incredulity.

'Don't worry,' Bharath thumped him on his back, 'we will protect you.'

If the fire officer had any fears of his safety, they evaporated when he looked around at the team of heavily armed, masked commandos in full battle gear and black balaclavas drawn over their faces.

Sharma's walkie-talkie crackled as he was convincing Kadam to go with them. His task force had arrived. He walked back to the Trident driveway to meet them. Unseen by the media, Sharma noted with satisfaction. A perfect stealth entry. The troopers alighted from their vehicle and fell in.

There was Captain Karamjeet Singh Yadav, an artillery officer who had been in the NSG for eighteen months. Captain A.K. Singh, lean and bespectacled, was in charge of the four-man sniper detachment. The commandos were accompanied by Major Saurabh Shah, Col Rathee's staff officer from the NSG's force headquarters. Sharma quickly passed his orders. The commandos were handed out one photograph each of the two terrorists. These had been thoughtfully printed out by Captain Grover. The fifty Task Force Oberoi commandos were divided into two teams of twenty-five each: Team A under Lt Col Sharma and Team B under Major B. Bharath.

Captain A.K. Singh and his three-man sniper detachment, meanwhile, crossed the road towards the NCPA Towers that overshadowed the Oberoi. From their perches on this twenty-one-storey building, the snipers would cover the commandos.

Sharma knew room intervention would play a major part in the operation. It called for split-second judgement, especially when terrorists took shelter behind hostages. He could not afford mistakes. He told the officers to personally lead the room intervention teams. Major Shah volunteered to lead one of the teams. Time was of the essence. The commandos had to get to the terrorists before they killed their hostages.

The plan was for both teams to walk up to the roof of the Oberoi. From there, they would start the hazardous task of clearing over 300 rooms one by one. Three hit teams under Major Bharath, Major Saurabh Shah and Captain Karamjeet Singh Yadav were quickly formed. Captain A.K. Singh had 'sited' three snipers in an NCPA Towers flat facing the Oberoi. Exactly a year before, a four-bedroom apartment here had sold for a record 340 million rupees. Now, it was the only available perch from where snipers could cover the hotel. Not wanting to miss out on the action, Captain Singh had come back into the Oberoi and asked Col Rathee for permission to lead a house intervention team. He was now given charge of a fourth hit team. Lt Col Sharma would lead the fifth hit team when room intervention began inside.

From his cabin in the hotel basement, Commander Sushil Nagmote called in four of his security staff to tell the guests the commandos were coming. The security guards had to dial the phones in all the rooms and find out whether they were occupied. 'Let the phone ring five times, if there's no response, move on to the next room,' he told them in his gravelly voice. The guests were given Nagmote's phone numbers and asked to speak with him. Over the next few hours, they established contact with guests in twenty-five rooms. Fortunately, fewer than half of the 320 rooms of the Oberoi had been occupied the previous night. A majority of the guests were touring the city when the terrorists struck. A few had heard the grenade blasts and fled. Only a handful of guests remained – but their lives were in very real danger.

Nagmote explained the situation to the guests in the twenty-five rooms. NSG commandos are in the hotel, he told them. 'They are coming to rescue you. They are wearing black dungarees. Let them in after verifying from the peephole.' He advised the guests to lie on the floor next to the bed. They would not run out of drinking water, he assured them. 'The water in the bathroom is refined by our filtration plants. It's better than mineral water.'

Nearly two hours after he had first seen the hotels, Major Bharath, MP5 in his right hand, gingerly opened the door of the faintly lit stairwell. The hotel's emergency fire exit spiralled up to the twenty-first floor. Behind him were Lt Col Sharma and the commandos. They didn't know this was the route the terrorists had taken as they climbed up the hotel in search of hostages the previous night.

The commandos switched off their radio sets and climbed to the roof slowly and deliberately. The hit teams leapfrogged each other. One team moved up, held one side of the stairs and covered the corridor with their weapons. Then, the next team moved up ahead. All the fire-escape doors had push bars, which meant that they could be opened only from the hotel corridor, not the fire escape. A force sneaking up the fire escape would have no option but to break the door down and give itself away.

On the seventeenth floor, the commandos saw a crack in the fire escape door. It was slightly ajar, wide enough to stick a knife blade in. Sharma thought speedily. He directed two commandos to stand guard. 'Until the entire column moves up, shoot anything that comes through here,' he told them.

A macabre trail led the commandos to the spot of the previous night's slaughter. At first they saw scattered bullet holes on the ceiling of the stairs. 'Strange,' Sharma thought to himself, 'was there a firefight on the stairs?' Then a pair of broken spectacles. A shoe. A lady's slipper. A silk scarf. It all led upstairs. The commandos slowed down, then stopped altogether when they looked up. A bloodied hand hung limply from the staircase.

They had reached the twenty-first floor. It opened to a two-level elevator machinery room. The stairs telescoped into an iron ladder barely four feet wide and six feet long. There were rivulets of blood running down from the stairs above. Six bodies were heaped on top of each other. The terrorists had executed their hostages from point-blank range. There were bullet holes on the wall, and bullets had knocked the light bulb out.

The door to the roof was locked. The commandos did not want to blast the door down and give away their arrival. They decided to try another route and returned to the open door on the seventeenth floor. Rajesh showed the teams the way in through the door and onto the guest floor.

They now had a view of the Oberoi's pièce de résistance: the cavernous polygonal atrium. Over thirty rooms per floor were wrapped around this vertiginous space. The fibreglass skylight let natural light into the atrium. Standing there, the layout of the hotel became clearer to the commandos. If you treated the atrium as the face of a clock, there were three entry points onto each floor: fire exit stairs at five and ten o'clock and a set of service stairs behind the elevators at eight o' clock. Rajesh had led them up the fire escape at ten o'clock. Now the commandos moved clockwise around the corridor and circled the atrium as they headed for the service stairs at eight o'clock that led straight to the rooftop.

There was an eerie, muffled silence in the atrium, the silence that terror and the fear of death can bring. Nothing else was out of place. All the polished brown doors that led to the rooms were shut. Each floor had a three-foot-high wall that ran around the central space, made alternately of brick and glass partitions, the latter having tubular brass balustrades.

The commandos looked across the floor. They could see most of the rooms on their level and below. In a tactical situation, such a commanding view levelled the playing field between them and the terrorists. The black figures filed quietly along on the red-carpeted floor, briefly merging with the black granite cladding of the elevator area. A few minutes later they had entered the daylight of the rooftop.

The commandos scoured the rooftop for potential threats. The discovery of the bodies lent further urgency to the operation. Room intervention operations would need to start on the twenty-first floor immediately. 'I hope there are no Rubaiyas in these rooms,' Major Bharath thought to himself as he led his men downstairs, fingers around his MP5.

'Rubaiya' was a special three-foot-high red-and-blue target the NSG commandos practised their shooting skills on at Manesar: a commando shot the red outline of a gun-wielding terrorist who held the blue outline of 'Rubaiya Sayeed', the daughter of former home minister Mufti Mohammad Sayeed. She had been kidnapped by Kashmiri secessionists in 1989 and released in exchange for five jailed terrorists, before the NSG could rescue her.

Every commando fired over 2,000 rounds in training at the NSG's firing ranges, and all of them dreaded the Rubaiya. Among the NSG's toughest tests, which called for split-second decision-making skills. One wrong move could jeopardize a rescue mission. One wrong shot at the blue target meant a commando had failed his test. At the Oberoi, only the officers would make this call. They knew this as they walked downstairs to the twenty-first floor.

Room intervention started from one side of the floor. Commandos took position covering the three entrances that led into the floor. The house intervention teams moved into rooms that were opened with the master key that Rajesh carried. Among the rooms they searched was the Rs 250,000-a-night Kohinoor Suite that had hosted Bill Clinton and Michael Jackson. Now the commandos walked inside and swept the massive suite with their MP5s, searching the drawing room, bathrooms and attached spa.

However, the commandos quickly realized that the master key could open only a single lock. Most guests had double-locked their rooms. It was useless calling on guest phones. Nobody believed them.

The Black Cats stood outside and knocked on the doors to no avail. 'Open up please, we are the police. We have come to help.' The message was repeated in Hindi and English. The doors were almost never opened. At times they had to be blasted down. On the twentieth floor, the commandos tried opening the door to a room. It was locked from inside. They could hear muffled voices from within. The commandos affixed a small 4-gram patch of PEK, on the door and blasted the lock. Then they kicked the door open and tossed a stun grenade inside, which went off with a deafening crack and flash. Sharma and the commandos entered with their MP5s cocked. A shell-shocked guest stood in the corner. His eyes bulged in horror as he saw a masked man in black overalls move in his direction. He began shaking with fear. 'Why weren't you responding, sir?' Sharma asked the guest, lowering the balaclava from his mouth to speak. The guest did not reply, but the officer saw the answer in the mirror. A masked, heavily armed man in black was hardly reassuring to frightened survivors. Sharma rolled his mask up. It would stay there for the rest of the operation.

'Isn't there a key that can open both locks,' an exasperated Col Rathee asked Rajesh. The deputy force commander had been following the commandos at a safe distance as they cleared rooms. He was worried at the time it was taking. The hotel had only one such key, Rajesh knew, but it was with the general manager, Mohit Nirula. He agreed to fetch it. The young fire officer dialled Nirula as he sprinted down. The GM told him the master key was in the bedroom of his apartment on the twenty-fifth floor of the Trident. So, Rajesh ran back up the stairs of the Trident, used a master key to open the GM's apartment and located the special metal master key with twin magnetic strips. When he returned nearly an hour later, the commandos had two master keys. Two hit teams were formed with the keys. The rescue operations continued. They perfected a drill to clear rooms. One team would open the room, but leave the key outside and go in to search the room. The other team would take the key and go on to the next room.

'Sniper, shift one,' Bharath spoke into his walkie-talkie. This was the signal for the snipers at the NCPA Towers to move one floor below. Frightened guests were kept in a secured room in the corner of the floor, closest to a fire escape. They were moved downstairs with the commandos after a floor had been cleared.

Bharath locked the dozen guests inside and gave them a code. They were to open only if they heard one sharp knock on the door followed by three rapid knocks and the password 'commandos, open up'. They were calmed down, offered food, water and chocolates taken from the minibar.

Operations on the twentieth and nineteenth floors proceeded without event. They entered the room with their MP5s raised and levelled ahead, fingers on the trigger. They then moved from corner to corner to sweep the room, always under the assumption there were terrorists in each room. They checked the doors, the space under the beds, the curtains behind the panoramic sliding windows and finally the bathrooms, before they gave the room a clear sign. Each 300-sq. ft room had a bathroom to the right of the door. The bathtub inside lay parallel to the corridor. There was a double bed, a minibar, a study table, three chairs, a sofa and a centre table and a 21-inch flat screen television. The commandos drew the curtains over the windows to indicate the room had been cleared. It took them five to ten minutes to clear each room.

On a narrow passage behind the elevators on the nineteenth floor, the commandos discovered the bodies of three women hostages. One of them was Lo Hwei Yen, the Singaporean lawyer. The bodies of the three women lay on their side and formed a triangle. Bharath halted his men as he radioed the police on his set. 'Please send policemen to the nineteenth floor. Over.' A few minutes later, two police officers cautiously walked up to the commandos. 'We found them,' Bharath pointed at the bodies. 'We have not fired a single shot.' The policemen regarded him with befuddlement. Was this why they had been called all the way up in a terrorist-infested hotel? '*Sa'ab, aap jo bhi kar rahe hain … theek hai* (whatever you are doing is right),' they said and departed hastily. They did not move the bodies for fear of booby traps.

On the same nineteenth floor, the commandos came up against a locked room. From the NCPA Towers, the snipers recorded movement inside the room. '*Humko andar* movement *deekh raha hai*,' the snipers radioed in. The commandos fixed a 25-gram slab of explosive on the lock. It exploded with a loud bang, cutting a rectangle into the door. The team streamed into the room. 'Commandos … heads down, hands up,' one of them called as they entered the room. Inside was an elderly Australian couple shaken but relieved to see the commandos. They were safely escorted to the holding suite on that floor.

Rajesh, meanwhile, received a call from Commander Nagmote in the security room. A guest in a room on the fourteenth floor wanted his blood pressure medicine. Rajesh ran down the hotel to the security room in the basement. The hotel had kept the medicine in a white envelope. He ran back up the stairs and knocked on the door. The guest opened the door just a crack, grabbed the medicine and shut the door. He did not want to leave his room, evidently because he was too scared.

The commandos then walked down to the eighteenth floor. It was 5.30 p.m. They had swept over ninety rooms and rescued ten guests so far. Their movements were now fine-tuned to drill-like perfection. They had added a variation in the door-opening drill. As soon as the LED (Light Emitting Diode) in the automatic lock beeped green, the officer would shove the door wide open and point his weapon ahead into the room. This move would startle anyone hiding behind the door.

Four hit teams swiftly moved to the staircases and stood guard. The floor was secured. The sprightly Major Saurabh Shah led four commandos to commence room-clearing operations.

Exhaustion had begun setting in. Bharath had entered room 1857 and cleared it. He then handed out plums from a fruit basket and small bottles of water lying inside the room. The commandos poured the water down their parched throats.

There were two rooms to the left of the elevator and at the corner of the floor. Room 1856, like any other room, had a brown wooden door with an oval brass number plate. It stood at the head of a narrow passage which led to five other rooms – 1851 through 1855 – that were hidden from view behind the guest elevators.

Major Shah drew the master key out of his pocket and inserted it into the key slot. The tiny LED light on the door lock blinked, turned green and beeped. Shah then shoved the door forward. Crack! Crack! Crack! A burst of three AK-47 bullets hammered the bottom of the door. Fahadullah had been standing behind the door, his rifle ready and cocked. Shah had startled him. As Fahadullah fell back, his bullets punched and splintered the door. A bullet grazed Shah's toe. The sound of the shots rippled across the atrium. Instinctively, all the commandos on the floor spread out and took cover, standing with their backs pressed to the walls. 'Charlie Four to Team Leader, have made contact,' Shah shouted into his radio set.

The shooting had started.

The five officers covered various parts of the polygonal floor. Captain Yadav and two hit teams covered the area closest to the bank of elevators near the room; Major Shah stood in the corridor to the right; Captain A.K. Singh and Major Bharath covered the corridor across the atrium; and Lieutenant Col Sharma, the far end of the lift corridor. All their weapons pointed at Room 1856.

Fahadullah and Abdul Rehman fired their AK-47s, the bullets whistling and cracking across the corridor as they broke the sound barrier. Across the atrium, Rajesh and Major Bharath took shelter behind a four-foot-high wooden table used to hold flowers. Intermittently, they raised their heads to fire a few shots at the room. Just then, Bharath heard the crack of a bullet as it whizzed past and felt the sensation of a hard slap. The bullet had split his ear in two. His ear went numb. Blood poured onto his black uniform. Bharath cupped his left hand over his ear, it was filled with blood.

'Bharath!' A.K. Singh whispered, '*khoon beh raha hai* (you're bleeding).'

'*Abbey, khoon nahin toh kya paani niklega* (What, you think I'll bleed water?),' he said drily. With that, Bharath pulled out a white field-dressing pack out of his pocket and put it on his ear. The white bandages were quickly filled with blood. He needed medical attention to stop the bleeding, and so walked down to the lobby, hand cupping the ear. Saurabh Shah volunteered to accompany him.

Meanwhile, the fusillade of bullets from the room had bent the brass balustrade and shattered the glass below it. The terrorists were cornered, but they would not go down without a fight. They opened the door of the room to fire and toss grenades at the commandos. Their 'fire discipline' surprised the commandos. The two men inside fired only single shots and they kept 'jockeying' or switching their firing position. Two shots rarely came from the same location. Their room was a defender's delight, a natural pillbox that had evidently been chosen with care. It was set in the corner of a corridor, protected by the bulge of the elevators on the right. The door was set at least four feet inside the wall, protected by the rooms on the left.

The commandos, on the other hand, had a restricted field of fire. Rajesh, who had taken cover, understood why the terrorists had chosen the Oberoi and not the Trident for the siege. The Oberoi, with its atrium and multiple exits, offered them many more options to do battle with the security forces.

With Bharath and Saurabh Shah gone, Captain A.K. Singh crawled up towards the room. A grenade flew out of the room in his direction. It exploded in the air. One steel splinter hit his left eye. Blood gushed out of the wound. Singh cupped his eye and gritted his teeth in pain. He lost sight in that eye. Subedar Dig Ram and Havildar Vikram shot out of cover and rushed him downstairs for medical attention. A second officer had been injured.

It was now past 6 p.m. and darkness had set on the city. The Oberoi had no lighting. It slowed down the operation. Sharma decided to blast open the door of the room that the terrorists were in a position to open at will. He called in the engineer commandos and directed Captain Yadav to provide them with covering fire.

Captain Yadav crawled close to 1856. From here, he provided cover fire to engineer commandos who placed the charge on the door of the room. An explosion partially splintered the door. As soon as the door was breached, Captain Yadav closed in and lobbed grenades into the room. There was an ear-splitting explosion. The firing from within the room subsided. The commandos kept lobbing stun grenades into the room.

The firefight between the commandos and terrorists gained momentum. The dull subsonic sounds of the MP5, like a coconut hitting the floor versus the AK-47's firecracker sound. The sounds echoed through the atrium. In the hotel, the remaining guests cowered in fear.

In their room on the twelfth floor, Bagla and Michael Queen heard a woman call for help. The muffled cries continued through the day, grew progressively weaker and finally stopped. Bagla had kept his Blackberry charged and within reach. It was his lifeline to the outside world – his wife and two sons in Delhi. On the morning of 27 November, he wept when he called his parents in New Delhi and whispered to them that he was trapped in Mumbai. Alive and safe. His mother Uma Bagla dropped the phone in shock when she heard where he was. His father, S.P. Bagla, a deeply spiritual seventy-five-year-old retired IAS officer, was philosophic: 'God will be with you. He will protect you.'

Bagla and Queen already feared the worst when their TV set had gone on the blink that morning. Hotel security had heeded the NSG's advice and snapped the cable connections. Their phones, where messages poured in from friends and family, were their only lifelines. Friends kept round-the-clock vigil for Bagla near the hotel and held prayer meets. In the darkened room, the two colleagues spoke in whispers about their families, mortality and what they could have done to prepare for eventualities like these.

Bharath, meanwhile, crossed the hotel lobby that smelt of stale air of death mixed with air freshener. The bodies had been removed, but the signs of violence, the black pools of blood on the red granite floor, were everywhere. He walked into an ambulance parked outside the hotel. A team of ten medical assistants fussed over his ear.

'We will have to stitch your ear up,' a doctor said grimly. 'Six stitches.'

'Six stitches?' the officer asked incredulously. 'Like embroidery? Patch it up, I need to go back up.' With Bharath's left ear swathed in white bandages, he and Shah walked back up the fire escape.

In the stairwell, Shah and Bharath heard footstep-like sounds. Klump ... klump ... They crouched in the corridor and drew their weapons. The fire escape was dark. Bharath pulled out his walkie-talkie and used the glow of its screen to read the floor number. It was the fourteenth floor. Bharath peeped out, pointed his carbine out and smiled. It was the sound of water droplets seeping from the top floors onto the carpets below. The officers continued their trudge up the stairs.

Col Rathee was waiting for him. 'Bharath, there's a senior officer on the line who wants to speak to you.' The young officer put the walkie-talkie over his right ear. It was Major General Hooda, the GOC who was calling the NSG from the communications centre they had set up in the hotel lobby.

'Sir, I am the squadron commander in charge of operations … pass.'

'Son,' Major General Hooda's voice, laced with concern even over the crackle of the radio, came on, 'what is the situation?'

'Sir, we have been able to establish contact … we will be able to neutralize them … pass.'

'Son, it's around 5.30 p.m. … can I tell the media that you will be through with the operations by 7 p.m.?'

Bharat gritted his teeth hard. 'Sir,' he said slowly, 'there are eleven floors … thirty-two rooms on each floor … we will not stop till we have cleared all of them … please don't be surprised if the operation continues for two days. Out.'

With that, he went back into the fight. Junior officers don't generally 'out' a senior officer. The polite word is 'over'. The GOC had struck a raw nerve.

The commandos kept firing at the door to keep the terrorists from breaking out. But they began running low on ammunition. Sharma sent Major Bharath – now returned, with what looked like a cauliflower on his left

cocktails. The Molotov cocktails improvised by the local military unit – beer bottles filled with a mixture of fuel oil and petrol – could be a crude but effective way of burning down the door. When his officer returned an hour later, he handed the Molotov cocktail to Captain Yadav and asked him to toss it inside. Captain Yadav lit the wick and flung it at the door. The cocktail crashed through the gap in the door and set Room 1856 on fire. The curtains obscuring the view from the rear burnt away. Black smoke billowed out of the room. The fire also triggered off the hotel's sprinkler system. Water spurted out of spouts in the ceiling, extinguishing the fire and giving a clear view of the room to the snipers positioned at NCPA Towers.

The NSG's snipers from the NCPA Towers began firing their aimed single shots at Fahadullah and Abdul Rehman. The two terrorists, rushed into the bathroom for shelter. The commandos lobbed more grenades into the room but these proved ineffective. The terrorists had a hideaway within a hideaway: the bathroom. They now opened the faucets in the bathroom. Water filled the bathtub, spread out into the room and gushed into the corridor outside.

Meanwhile, the two terrorists had a conversation with their handlers in Pakistan. It came about in an interesting manner. Lisa Ringner, a Swedish national and a nursing student in Mumbai's K.B. Bhabha Municipal Hospital, had been staying in Room 1856. She had been alerted by shots fired the previous evening and fled the hotel. The move saved her life. But she had left her cellphone behind in the room. Fahadullah now used the phone to call Wasi, his handler in Pakistan. The handler motivated his charge to keep fighting.

> *Wasi: The manner of your death will instil fear in the unbelievers. This is a battle between Islam and the unbelievers. Keep looking for a place to die. Keep moving.*
>
> *Fahadullah: Insha'allah.*
>
> *Wasi: You're very close to heaven now. One way or another we've all got to go there. You will be remembered for what you've done here. Fight till the end. Stretch it out as long as possible.*

The firefight and the water had turned the area around the room into a slushy puddle. The grenade blasts knocked the light fittings out in front of the room and lift area. They smashed the plaster of Paris false ceiling to reveal a thick mass of black electrical cables. Cable TV routers and wires hung limply like creepers. The corridor filled with half an inch of water, turning the red carpet into a soaking bog.

The commandos now planned to blow the outer bathroom wall. P.V. Manesh an engineer commando was tasked with planting an explosive. As he crouched and placed a charge on the bathroom wall, one of the terrorists flung a grenade at him. The grenade exploded on Manesh's head. It tore his steel helmet. Steel fragments from the shattered helmet dug into his skull. Manesh staggered to the corridor and fell. Captain Yadav pulled the wounded commando away to the safety of another part of the corridor. Manesh's injuries seemed grievous; it did not look like he would survive. There was a temporary pause in operations as the commandos tended their wounded comrade.

The commandos had, however, killed one of the terrorists. At around 8 p.m. Indian intelligence agencies intercepted a phone conversation between Fahadullah and Wasi.

Wasi: How are you, my brother?

Fahadullah (sounding weak): Praise God. Brother Abdul Rehman has passed away.

Wasi: Really? Is he near you?

Fahadullah: Yeah, he's near me.

Wasi: May God accept his martyrdom.

Fahadullah: The room is on fire. I'm sitting in the bathroom.

Wasi: Don't let them arrest you. Don't let them knock you out with a stun grenade. That would be very damaging. Fire one of your magazines, then grab the other one and move out. The success of your mission depends on your getting shot.

It was half past midnight on 28 November. Electricity to the hotel had been restored. The lights burnt weakly through the corridors. Room 1856 and its vicinity resembled a coal pit. The fire had charred the whitewashed walls around the room. The corridor was indistinguishable from the black granite facade of the elevators. Sharma was on guard at the fire exit near five o'clock. Havildar Somappa Kedari and Rajesh Kadam were with him. Rajesh sat on the floor, his long legs stretched out on the carpet. A four-foot-high housekeeping trolley stood next to him. He was dazed. The firing and explosions had numbed him. It was the thought of seeing his wife Sujata, then seven months pregnant with their first child, that kept him going. Sharma took stock of the situation. Four commandos were injured, two of them severely. His force on the eighteenth floor had thinned out. He had to regroup and launch another assault on the room.

Then a short burst of AK fire echoed through the atrium. It was difficult to tell the source but the gunfire did not come from within the room. It was in the atrium. 'Who's firing?' Sharma wondered. Was it the marine commandos or the Mumbai police? Had one of his commandos cracked under pressure? There was a second burst. This time very close to where he stood. The bullets drilled the wall and blasted out puffs of white dust. '*Abbey paagal ho gaya hai kya?* (Idiot, have you gone mad?),' Sharma yelled as he darted back into the corridor for cover.

The figure fired again, this time from within the narrow niche of the elevator door. Still unsure about the identity of the shooter, Sharma raised his MP5, but Havildar Somappa Kedari held him back. 'Sahab,' he shouted frantically. 'The man is in black. It could be our commando.'

The figure continued to fire and move towards them. Sharma shot a glance out of his cover. It was Fahadullah. He had taken advantage of the lull in the fighting and broken out of the room, determined to shoot his way out. Sharma's thumb slipped his MP5 selector to a three-round burst. Sharma aimed and fired two quick bursts. The MP5 rattled. Fahadullah was hit in the leg. He staggered and limped back towards the elevators. Enraged, Fahadullah screamed, '*Chhup chhup ke wahan se kya maar raha hain, agar dum hain to saamne aakar lad* (Why do you shoot hidden there. If you dare, come out and fight).'

Sharma shouted back: '*Agar tujhme zyaada dum hai to tu saamane kyon nahi aata?* (If you're so strong, why don't you come forward?)'

A tense stand-off ensued. Both held their positions. Sharma had run out of ammunition. He had to stop the militant from slipping out in the dark towards the other side of the corridor. He quietly reached out for his radio set and whispered to Bharath: 'This is Charlie One. Arrange for ammunition, searchlight and bamboo sticks. Proceed on the double.'

It was around 2.30 a.m. on Friday, 28 November. Bharath arrived with boxes of 9 mm ammunition from the Mumbai police, and Sharma asked him to fling a grenade at the terrorist from the nineteenth floor. Sharma and Kedari, refilled their weapons with the ammunition and shot at Fahadullah. Bharath ran up to the nineteenth floor. He had just one HE 36 hand grenade left – he had to make it count. Fahadullah kept firing single shots, inaccurately, from his hideout in the elevator passageway. Clearly, he was wounded. Bharath pulled the pin on the grenade and lobbed it into the corridor. It exploded. Fahadullah stopped firing.

At dawn, light streamed into the atrium. At around 7 a.m., on 28 November, close to fourteen hours after they had first made contact, Bharath spotted the body of the terrorist lying in the corridor. He aimed his MP5 and fired once at it. No movement. The commandos walked down the corridor. Fahadullah lay dead on his back on the floor near the elevators, eyes vacantly staring. His AK-47, two magazines and a pistol lay beside him. Empty cartridges lay around. His right hand had only a thumb and forefinger.

Room intervention operations resumed to clear the left corridor and secure the eighteenth floor. Captain Yadav swung open what was left of the door to Room 1856. The room was a compact battle zone. The terrorists had used the room's two doors as a barrier. They had used the minibar and a study table as firing positions. Yadav stepped on hundreds of AK-47 brass empties. The windows and the bed and a sofa were half burnt. The carpeted floor was still soggy and strewn with shoes and clothes. Yadav aimed his weapon at the bathroom. The door was open. The second terrorist, Abu Rehman Chhota, lay on his back on the bathroom floor. A bullet had passed through his right eye. The room was clear.

The terrorists had been neutralized, but the operation did not end there. The NSG carried out room intervention operations in the rest of the hotel, moving from top downwards. Among the remaining guests to be rescued were Deepak Bagla and Michael Queen who had spent forty hours in their room. The Oberoi was eventually cleared of civilians. Bodies of the dead civilians were removed by 4.30 p.m. on 28 November. Guests from all floors were thoroughly screened again and handed over to the hotel authorities. The NSG's bomb disposal squad conducted their Render Safe Procedure, sweeping the hotel for live ordnance and ammunition, and searching for possible booby traps before the site was handed over to the hotel authorities. At 6.30 on the evening of 28 November, the commandos silently trooped into the lobby of the Trident. The lobby echoed with the sound of applause. Hotel staff queued up to look at the men in black. The officers walked into the porch where two black Mercedes stood in the driveway. It was to be their transport to the Taj hotel.

Captain Yadav nudged Bharath and gave him a small greeting card. Bharath opened it and laughed heartily. 'Life is too short,' Yadav had scribbled on it. 'Two inches short.'

Task Force Nariman House

Twelve hours after terrorists had laid siege to Mumbai, Lt Col Sundeep Sen stood on the tarmac at the IGI airport, New Delhi, and inspected the cargo hold of an IL-76. His troopers had loaded it exactly the way the NSG flight had been the previous night. Weapons under a netting in the centre, soldiers on the sides. It was, in fact, the same aircraft that had returned from Mumbai, quickly refuelled and furnished with a fresh Aviation Research Centre crew in the cockpit.

A series of events had propelled Sen to the head of the SAG's Counter Terrorism Task Force-2 (CTTF-2). This sub-unit would normally be commanded by the deputy force commander, Col Rathee. But Rathee had left for Mumbai the night before. Sen was thus de facto head of CTTF-2. He knew, of course, that the impressive acronym masked an uncomfortable truth: the SAG's second strike force was effectively only a reserve unit. Most of the 148 personnel inside the IL-76 – fourteen officers, thirty junior commissioned officers (JCOs) and

104 commandos – did not sport the 'Balidaan' badge because they were still a month away from graduation day, the 'Balidaan parade'. Their weapons and equipment too were second-rate. Most wore their army fatigues and the Indian Army's Model 74 fibreglass helmet, which provided only moderate protection from shrapnel and none at all from bullets.

The previous night, Sen had packed off the best weapons and equipment and all the night-vision devices to CTTF-1. When it was time for the reservists, CTTF-2, to move, Sen scraped together all the leftover equipment to kit out his force. They had reached the NSG's headquarters opposite the IGI airport at 2.30 a.m. As day broke over Delhi five hours later, Col Pathania, the NSG's general staff officer (Operations), asked Sen to fly to Mumbai.

This was not CTTF-2's first deployment. When terrorists struck at Akshardham in 2002, CTTF-1 was away in the dense forests between Karnataka and Tamil Nadu on the trail of forest brigand Veerappan. The poacher had kidnapped former Karnataka state minister H. Nagappa. It was CTTF-2 that flew in to Ahmedabad to neutralize the terrorists.

Sen looked at his watch impatiently. The force had been waiting nearly an hour now for the NSG's IG (Operations) Major General Abhay Gupta to fly into the airport from Mussoorie. But the Mi-17 helicopter that was flying him in could not land at the IAF's Palam

Technical Area because of ground haze. It had been diverted to the IAF airbase at Hindon on the eastern outskirts of Delhi. A commando had taken the general's uniform and haversack to the IAF airbase. He changed into his black NSG uniform in the airbase and then drove 40 km to the ARC complex at IGI airport.

Sen was two officers short that morning. But Major Manish Mehrotra had raced back from a brief holiday in Gurgaon to rejoin his unit in Manesar a few hours ago. The other officer, Captain Mohit Dhingra, had implored him breathlessly half an hour ago, 'Sir, I'm on my way. Give me a few minutes.' Sen told him he couldn't wait even a minute. If he missed the aircraft, Mohit could stay behind and help at the headquarters. True to his word, Sen didn't wait. As soon as Major General Gupta boarded the IL-76, Sen looked at his wristwatch. It was 10 a.m. He gave the signal to leave. The IL-76's hydraulic ramp creaked shut. The crew ladder was pulled up and the high-pitched whine of the Gajraj's four engines began. Mohit was a dedicated, hard-working team player. Sen would miss him. The aircraft had begun taxiing past the line-up of ARC aircraft and towards the runway when Sen squinted out of the crew door and smiled.

He saw a black dungaree-clad figure swinging a haversack, sprinting down the tarmac. It was Mohit, running hell for leather. Sen passed instructions to the pilot to halt the aircraft. The giant aircraft shuddered to a stop. The crew ladder was lowered. Mohit clambered into the aircraft, panting. Tired and grateful, he slumped on a seat next to Major Manish Mehrotra. Major Mehrotra was the senior in the course but the two officers were already close friends. 'Were you really thinking of leaving without me,' he asked him in mock anger. 'Ha!' Major Manish snorted. 'Who do you think kept the door open for you?' Sen, meanwhile, walked over and thumped the young officer on his back.

The previous day, 26 November, had been a big one in Mohit's life. He had driven down with his fiancée Keshar to meet his parents in Dehra Dun in the evening. The two had met at a common friend's wedding in Pune four years ago and had been dating since then. His parents approved. Mohit was over the moon. He heard of the attacks after the family got home from dinner at around 11 p.m. and called his friend Major Unnikrishnan. Something told the officer he would be called in. Mohit took his car and covered the 287 km to Manesar at breakneck speed. He then ran to his room in the unit to pick up his alert bag before he looked for transport. Mohit spotted a car from the Special Ranger Group (SRG) and offered a unit driver a case of Old Monk rum if he got him to the ARC complex in half an hour. The driver took up the wager and delivered.

Now, Mohit sat inside the yellow interior of the densely packed cargo hold, looking for familiar faces. Most of them were from CC 73, the commando course he had completed a few months earlier. Among the veterans, he saw Havildar Gajender Singh Bisht, a commando from the 10 Parachute Special Forces battalion. It was Gajender's second NSG tenure. Mohit remembered him from his deployment at the Commonwealth Youth Games in Pune the previous month. Mohit had forgotten his boots. 'Sir, you can wear my shoes,' the tough JCO helpfully volunteered at the time. They both wore size eight. Mohit had declined, but hadn't forgotten the gesture. In the aircraft that morning, he noticed Gajender wore the same pair of black ankle-high sneakers.

The commandos would have to be launched immediately after reaching Mumbai, so they used the flight time to Mumbai to kit themselves out. They inserted plates into their bullet proof jackets, untied and tied their boot laces and carefully checked their sub-machine guns and pistols.

Sen, meanwhile, walked over and briefed his officers. Hostage situations seemed to be developing at the Taj and the Oberoi. The force would have to be extremely careful. 'Officers and JCOs will accompany their men at all times,' he instructed.

At around noon on Thursday, 27 November, Operation Black Tornado's second IL-76 flight landed at Mumbai's Chhatrapati Shivaji International Airport. It taxied past the rows of Gulfstreams and Falcons, the parking lot for the city's billionaires. As the ramp slowly swung down, the 150 uniformed men trudged purposefully down the ramp.

Nisar Tamboli stepped forward and greeted Sen, making polite conversation. 'Why are you carrying so much ammunition?' he asked.

'Because we have no backup,' Sen said, his voice mixed with pride and mild annoyance. 'If we fail, there is no one else.'

A dozen BEST buses had been parked close to the tarmac. The men quickly boarded them and loaded their equipment. Sen saw an informal reception committee, over a hundred persons, men, women, air-hostesses and other airlines employees, lining the airport tarmac. The women were shouting 'all the best'. Sen politely waved at them as he walked to a private taxi the police had brought along. He immediately dialled Brigadier Sisodia who instructed him to head for Mantralaya.

At 3 p.m., DGP Anami Roy briefed Major General Gupta and Lt Col Sen about the situation at Nariman House. The team had to shed personnel for the Taj operation. So the main task force was further divided into two groups. That morning, Brigadier Sisodia had already conducted a recce of Nariman House. He had asked Sheoran for commandos. Although the colonel informed him he couldn't spare any, he deputed a recce group with the brigadier.

TARGET : NARIMAN HOUSE

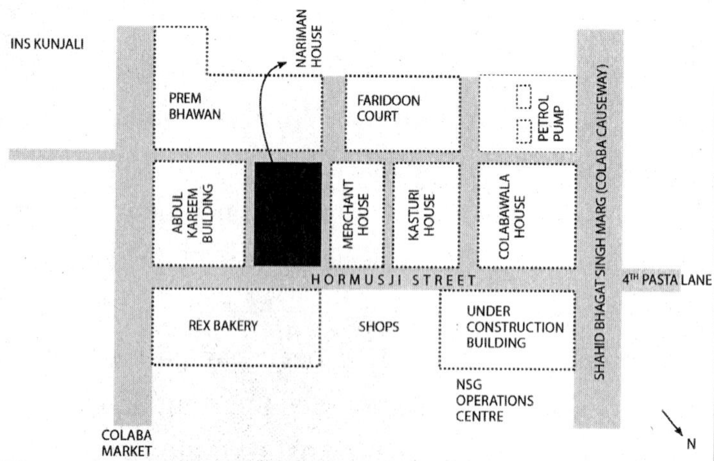

India's landmark hotel was the first priority for the NSG. The operation there was swallowing up personnel. Over a hundred NSG commandos were already deployed. More men were required to rescue guests. Sisodia directed Sen to immediately rush fifty troopers to the Taj operation. He asked him to take the remaining personnel to storm Nariman House.

Sen was now effectively controlling a front-line unit. He then understood the terrorists' game plan. They had known the NSG's vulnerability. They could not address more than a single location. And how could they? The half-century history of global terrorism had never witnessed multiple sieges.

'But why would they capture a residential apartment?' Sen wondered. Perhaps, like Ismail Khan and Kasab who went on a carjacking rampage, these terrorists too had lost their way. 'Could they have strayed into a civilian area and taken hostages?'

The unit had no night-vision devices, which meant they could only fight during the day. Sen deputed Major Manish Mehrotra to lead the assault. Mohit would be in reserve. 'Sir,' Mohit said, visibly dejected, 'what's the point of my coming and joining the unit if I don't get a chance?' Sen thought for a minute and nodded. Mohit was back in the squad.

banking firm Tower Capital and Securities Private Ltd, rented the apartment on the third floor of Merchant House, within hand-shaking distance of Nariman House. His landlord, Manoj Merchant was the oldest of a family of three Gujarati garment trader brothers, who owned the building. The youngest, Sushil Merchant and his wife Rita lived on the first floor and his older brother Lalit Merchant and his wife Chanda on the second floor. Muscular and clean-shaven, head and all, Bharadwaj, thirty-eight, had returned home the previous evening after a heavy workout at a neighbouring gym. He had not had time to shower and quickly donned cargo trousers and a T-shirt. His British-born wife, Lucy Varley, was to board a 1 a.m. flight to London. Lucy, forty, who worked as a research language editor with a city-based securities firm, was looking forward to meeting her mother Amanda who lived in London. The couple had met and married in the UK a decade ago when Bharadwaj was studying for his MBA at the Manchester Business School. Tonight, the cabbie who was to pick her up had lost his way. Bharadwaj was on the phone directing the cabbie when a hail of bullets forced him to dart inside. At around 10 p.m., a massive blast threw Bharadwaj off his sofa and onto the floor. It was the IED the terrorists had planted at the petrol pump behind their home. The apartment's huge French windows shattered and covered the floor of their home with glass shards. The front door hung from its hinges. The couple retreated into a tiny bathroom.

They pulled out a quilt and lay down; they would spend a terrifying twelve hours on the cold, damp floor. There was intermittent firing every half-hour. The couple winced as they heard the screams of the hostages being tortured by the terrorists. Lucy reached up to the counter and picked out two large kitchen knives and kept it beside them. She had been a reservist with the British Territorial Army while in college. Her training began to kick in.

Each time the terrorists fired a shot, the crows in the area would caw loudly. This stop-start avian cacophony added to the eeriness. The couple had two gas cylinders in the kitchen directly in the line of fire. 'We can't sit here for long, if a bullet hits the cylinders, it'll be like a bomb going off,' Bharadwaj whispered to his wife.

Then, everything was quiet in the morning. 'I want my tea ...' Lucy whispered into his ear. Bharadwaj woke up with a start. 'No terrorist is stopping me from my tea.' She reached into the laundry basket and tore up a T-shirt, then tied it around her knees and elbows and did an infantry low crawl across the glass-strewn floor to the refrigerator around ten feet away. She came back with a kettle and a tetrapack of milk and oats for her husband. Bharadwaj pulled himself together and dialled Puran Doshi, the former corporator with a desperate plea for help. 'Can you ask the police to rescue us?' Doshi was sitting with ACP Issaq Bagwan just then and passed the phone on to him. Bagwan said he could not send any policemen. The situation was extremely dangerous.

A few minutes later, Bharadwaj received a flurry of phone calls from TV channels. 'You are in Merchant House; tell us what it feels like?' Fatigued and sleep-deprived as he was, Bharadwaj feigned ignorance. 'I'm not in Mumbai, don't disturb me,' he mumbled. One of the reporters, however, was insistent he speak from his hiding place. 'Do you want to get me killed?' Bharadwaj whispered. 'The terrorists are just eight feet away from me.' The journalist backed off but on condition that Bharadwaj give him the first interview after his rescue.

Bharadwaj turned his ire on the former corporator Doshi. 'I asked you for help, instead you are having me killed,' he said. Doshi protested his innocence. Bharadwaj was unconvinced.

were also busy on their phones. They were in contact with Professor P.V. Viswanath, an Indian-born finance professor from the Lubin School of Business in Pace University, New York. The professor was a devout Jew who spoke Hebrew and Urdu, had been roped in by the Chabad-Lubavitch authorities in New York to try and communicate with the terrorists. This unusual channel had been established when one of the Chabad authorities had called on Rabbi Holtzberg's phone that morning. Babar Imran had answered it. He now demanded to be put in touch with the Indian authorities and wanted the captured terrorist Ajmal Kasab to be released in exchange for his Jewish prisoners. The negotiations were fruitless. In the chaos that followed the attacks, the Chabad negotiators were bounced from one Indian government office to another. The terror masterminds were, however, not serious about negotiations.

At around 7.45 a.m. Imran's Karachi-based handler Sajid Mir who used the alias Wassi rang Babar Imran's cellphone.

Wassi: Keep in mind that the hostages are of use only as long as you don't come under fire, because of their safety. If you are threatened, don't saddle yourself with the burden of the hostages. Immediately kill them.

Babar Imran: Yes, we shall do accordingly, God willing.

Wassi: The army claims to have done the work without any hostage being harmed. Another thing, Israel has made a request through the diplomatic channels to save the hostages. If the hostages are killed, it will spoil relations between India and Israel.

Babar Imran: So be it, God willing.

Wassi: Stay alert.

Nariman House was less than 2 km down the road from the Colaba police station. Lt Col Sen had visited the station for intelligence, but it was a picture of chaos. A local youth, who was at the police station, guided the NSG officer to the scene of the siege. It was 4.30 p.m. when Sen reached Nariman House. The shops along Colaba Causeway had not reopened that day and the road was closed for regular traffic, but it buzzed with thousands of people who had spilled out of homes. The area had been cordoned off by loose groups of khaki-clad policemen and Rapid Action Force (RAF) personnel clad in their distinctive blue camouflage uniform. Sen had expected a curfew. Instead, he saw surging crowds and media. A larger force of policemen controlled this curious mob. He was aghast. A terror attack had become a public spectacle. His officers, Manish and Mohit, who had reached Nariman House at 3 p.m., were on the ground and doing a detailed recce.

Nariman House was located less than 100 feet into Hormusji Street just off Colaba Causeway. It was the third building down the narrow street, after the under-construction Kasturi building and the three-storeyed Merchant House. The three buildings stood side by side, and Merchant House shared a boundary wall with the other two. The street was barely wide enough for a car to drive through. Nariman House stood out as a neat cream-coloured construction in the Colaba Market area, a densely packed urban sprawl of over 200 three- and four-storeyed old buildings inhabited by over 40,000 middle-class people.

The Mumbai police had pulled out civilians from these buildings in the initial hours following the attack, but gave up and withdrew after the terrorist gunfire became incessant and dangerous. Civilians were still trapped, vulnerable to gunfire and collateral damage from the NSG operation. It was not just Nariman House, police and locals at the site told Sen. Terrorists were also ensconced in the three-storeyed Merchant House. There was no response from any of the three families that lived on each floor of the building. The police had attempted to enter Kasturi building, but AK-47 fire from the terrorists on the rooftop of the Nariman House, had prevented them. Three bystanders had already died on the streets the previous evening.

There were at least four attackers, the police informed Sen. They kept up a steady fusillade of bullets from several windows in both buildings. Bullet holes pockmarked the exteriors of both. Part of the boundary wall and sliding iron gate at Nariman House had collapsed. A pile of bricks marked an exposed stairwell that had been blasted away by terrorists the previous night. A carpet of glass shards blasted out of the windows during the previous night's gunfight now covered the pavement outside the building. It alerted the terrorists to anyone approaching.

Brigadier Sisodia's sniper and surveillance detachment, comprising one shooter with a PSG-1 rifle and two spotters with a radio set, on the fifth floor of an under-construction building diagonally opposite Nariman House were at a disadvantage. They could not see inside the building. The curtains on the upper floors of Nariman House had been drawn. All its windows were covered by a screen of simple horizontal wrought-iron grills that resembled a rocket-propelled grenade (RPG) cage around US Stryker armoured personnel carriers. The commandos would find it difficult to enter through those windows.

The first thing they needed was an operations centre. Sen and his officers located a forty-foot-wide space between two single-storeyed buildings, less than 100 metres away from Nariman House. This space, ringed with bicycles, small water cisterns and sleeping cots, was a common courtyard for several one-room tenements called chawls in Mumbai. From here they could see the top two floors of Nariman House. NSG officers requisitioned three charpoys. A wood-topped metal office table, hastily covered with a bed sheet, was placed in front of a dirty yellow wall scrawled with graffiti that advertised a somewhat dubious massage. The officers sat on six plastic chairs. This was the makeshift operations centre of India's most formidable anti-terrorist force.

The NSG team identified five escape routes out of Nariman House. Bags of flour borrowed from a nearby grocery store were pressed into service as improvised sandbags blocking these escape routes. Ten commandos in buddy pairs were posted as 'stops' with local armed police units.

Sen needed to know more about the building's layout before he sent his men in. Specifically, how many flats per floor and how many doors and windows each flat had. Sen was clear about one thing: he would not send his men in blind.

At the makeshift control centre, Major General Gupta, Major Mehrotra and Captain Dhingra racked their brains.

Nariman House posed a problem. Locals rarely visited the house. Externally, the building appeared to have two flats per floor. Local residents brought in a mason who had done some repairs inside the building. The mason squatted on the street and drew a rough sketch. But a few queries from the officers made it clear that the workman was confused.

The NSG's trump card was simultaneous multiple entries. Commandos would blast down doors and walls to enter a room. They would then use their reflex shooting skills to nail the gunmen before they could harm the hostages. All this in less than a minute. This 'intervention technique' assumed one critical precept: negotiations with the terrorists were ongoing. Negotiations bought time. The commandos spent this time to glean intelligence about a building, rehearse on mock-ups of the target and, when the green signal was given, storm the building using the element of surprise. It was not a unique method. Every hostage situation from Entebbe in 1976 to Islamabad's Lal Masjid siege in 2007 used this technique.

There were two persons who could have provided a window into Nariman House: Sandra Samuel, the nanny of the Holtzbergs' two-year-old son Moshe, and Qazi Zakir 'Jackie' Hussein, the Holtzbergs' cook. Sandra and Hussein had remained hidden in the pantry of the first floor when the shooting started. At 11 a.m. that day, the two had slipped out of the building. Then, hearing the cries of the child on the floor above, Sandra had in an act of exceptional courage, gone back upstairs, picked up the toddler and run out of the ruined building cradling him in her arms. The NSG commandos weren't aware that the duo had been whisked away to the Colaba police station.

The commandos also did not know of the brief attempt by the terrorists in Nariman House to negotiate the release of Ajmal Kasab. But these were only the first of many gaps in information sharing that would become painfully apparent as the operation at Nariman House began.

Then Brigadier Sisodia arrived from the Taj and accompanied Lt Col Sen to INS *Kunjali*, the naval air station less than 500 metres away from Nariman House. Accompanied by local corporator Vinod Shekhar, Sen and Sisodia circled the area in a naval helicopter. The corporator pointed out the location of Nariman House from the air. The officers quickly took stock of what it would need to assault the building.

By 6.30 p.m. that day, the NSG had established its inner cordon and snipers. Four sniper detachments took position in four buildings around Nariman House. They would shoot the terrorists if they attempted to fire at the commandos. But they were severely handicapped. They could still not see inside the building. They could not fire and risk shooting hostages. The shadows around Colaba were already lengthening by the time Sen told

General Gupta of his plan: 'Sir, we'll start the operation tomorrow morning.' Gupta agreed. Meanwhile, the commandos would clear the buildings in the periphery of civilians to ensure zero civilian casualties. The first building to be evacuated was the six-storey Prem Bhawan that stood directly behind Nariman House. Having successfully evacuated the building, two commando squads headed into the under-renovation building swathed in blue plastic sheets and extricated a family of seven construction workers who had been trapped there when the firing began.

Around 9.30 p.m. on Thursday, 27 November, nearly twenty-four hours after it had been attacked, electricity supply to Nariman House was cut off. The house was illuminated only by the ghostly glow of the floodlights outside. A five-man probe made its way to Nariman House. The boots of the commandos scrunched the shattered glass. Almost on cue, a grenade dropped out of the window into the narrow gap between the building and the compound wall. It exploded on the red, paved parking lot, the steel ball bearings stitching a lethal pattern on the wall. The NSG withdrew. The sole ground approach into the building was a kill zone. The building was essentially a six-storey concrete bunker with only one approach: the rooftop.

At around 10 p.m., Indian intelligence picked up this ominous exchange between terrorists in Nariman House and their handlers in Karachi.

Sajid Mir (to other handlers): Do you want to keep the hostages or kill them?

Voice in the background: Kill them.

Sajid Mir: Listen up …

Babar Imran: Yes, yes …

Sajid Mir: Get rid of them. Firing could start on you at any time and you risk leaving them behind …

Babar Imran: Insha'allah, there is no movement from my side now …

Sajid Mir: No, don't wait any longer … you never know when the firing starts and what intensity it will be … just make sure you prop them up against a door and that the bullet doesn't ricochet from a wall …

Babar Imran: Insha'allah, Insha'allah …

Sajid Mir: I'm keeping on hold. Go on, do it, do it. I'm listening … do it …

Babar Imran: Yes. Do it. Sit them up, put their heads facing forward and keep the gun at the back of their heads.

Babar Imran: The thing is that Umar isn't feeling too well … I thought I would sleep for some time.

Sajid Mir: I'll call you in half an hour. Then you can do it.

An hour later.

Sajid Mir: Yes, brother …

Babar Imran: Don't be angry, had to move things around a bit …

Sajid Mir: Have you done the job or not?

Babar Imran: Now. In front of you … I was waiting for your call so that I would do it before you …

Sajid Mir: Do it in the name of God.

Babar Imran: Yes, hold …

Sajid Mir: Do it in the name of God …

[The sound of a gunshot]

Sajid Mir: That was one of them?

Babar Imran: Both of them. Together.

This conversation did not reach the NSG in time.

assault. They needed twenty men skilled in slithering down a helicopter. Not all the NSG personnel were qualified, so the officers selected only those who had had done some slithering in the past. Their canvas bags held the ropes already – several metres of special polyester abseil ropes designed for rapid descent from helicopters, rock faces and in urban warfare situations. But where were the large oven-mitt-sized gloves? Without them, a rapid descent down the ropes would shear the skin off a commando's palms.

Mohit discovered that the gloves were lying with the commandos in the Taj. He immediately deputed a two-man team to the hotel to locate them. The troopers returned an hour later. The hotel was in a state of chaos. There were hundreds of vehicles of multiple agencies parked there. The gloves simply could not be located. Mohit put his hands on his hips, gritted his teeth and looked down, as was his habit when he was thinking hard. Then he looked around. His eyes fell on the jute bags. They would have to do. 'Let's improvise,' he said. One group of NSG personnel used knives to cut the bags up into gloves and used needles and thread from their alert bag to stitch them up. At the end of an hour, the team was gloved.

Mohit then joined Manish's search of the buildings in the vicinity. Now, only Merchant House remained.

Sandeep Bharadwaj's phone blinked.

'This is Major Manish Mehrotra of the NSG,' the voice at the other end said. 'I have come to help. Where are you?'

'I'm in the bathroom on the second floor,' Bharadwaj whispered.

'Switch your light on,' Mehrotra said.

'I will flick the light switch on for just a minute,' Bharadwaj replied.

The NSG official saw Bharadwaj's brief light signal. 'Ok, I see you … wait, we're coming to get you.'

Bharadwaj crawled out of his hiding spot. Havildar Gajender Singh waved at him. The commandos had wedged an old door from Kasturi building as a makeshift bridge to Merchant House. Gajender Singh had sawed off the grille of a window in Kasturi building with his dagger. It had taken him nearly three hours to cut through. Power tools and gas cutters could alert the terrorists, then believed to be in both the buildings. Bharadwaj's kitchen window fortunately did not have grilles. The commandos led by Major Mehrotra used the bridge to enter the Bharadwaj residence. The couple's agony had ended. The operation to clear Merchant House then hit an unexpected two-hour delay. The Merchant brothers on the first and second floors refused to open doors to their apartments and refused to answer telephone calls. Manish and Mohit were prepared to blow their doors down. 'If they don't open the doors, we have to assume there are terrorists inside,' Manish said. They, however, decided to try the phone lines again.

Lalit Merchant was finally persuaded to open the door of his second-floor flat. He shuffled out, silent and in a state of shock. His wife Chanda, barely five feet tall, sobbed without respite. The commandos who escorted the couple up the stairs had to beg her to keep quiet lest they alerted the terrorists. After nearly an hour, his youngest brother Sushil Merchant finally answered his phone. I cannot leave the house, he told the commandos,

I have cash and jewellery. 'You can enjoy it only if you are alive,' Manish told him. Sushil Merchant opened his door at last. His wife Rita, a heavy-set homemaker, wore a maroon saree and held a brown plastic bag to her bosom. It held the family's cash and valuables. The third occupant of the flat was their son Mitesh, twenty-three. The two families were taken upstairs for evacuation through the makeshift bridge in the Bharadwaj residence. Commandos stood on both sides to help them cross the ten-foot-wide bridge. When Rita Merchant's turn came, she refused to leave her bag. 'Madam, you need to keep both your hands free to cross over,' Manish cajoled her. She reluctantly gave him the bag to cross over but ensured it was quickly passed back to her.

It was 1 a.m. on 28 November. Manish, Mohit and their teams had by now pulled out a dozen families and nearly sixty persons to safety from three buildings. Now, their target, Nariman House, stood isolated and bathed in spotlight.

Mohit radioed the completion of the evacuation to Sen. By now the NSG officer had figured out why the police had initially overestimated the number of terrorists. They changed positions while firing from the windows in the building: a technique called jockeying. It was a simple trick that created the illusion of greater numbers. The terrorists fired only single shots to conserve ammunition.

Around 1.15 a.m., Captain Kush Kashyap, deployed at one of the stops below Nariman House, reported a woman's cry. It was a piercing shriek which one of the officers mistook for that of a child. The team commanders rushed to the location of the stop and carried out a listening drill. The cry came from within Nariman House. The commandos could not determine where she was. Sen and his officers then trudged up to all the four sniper perches to locate the militants in the building. The house was absolutely still. No one could be seen except the brief blurry outlines of militants, who kept firing single shots at regular intervals until 4.30 a.m.

From the kitchen of Sandeep Bharadwaj's flat, Sen managed to peep into the second floor of Nariman House. He could make out the faint outline of a body lying facedown on the floor of the house. The situation was desperate, he realized. They had started killing hostages. 'Is there anybody inside?' Sen shouted from the roof of Merchant House. 'Please shout, tell us you are alive.' There was silence.

The NSG finally decided to storm the building from the rooftop at dawn, now only a few hours away. At 5 a.m., Sen briefed his men – the twenty NSG personnel who would go in for the operation – on the rooftop of Merchant House. The force was divided into four squads. Captain Mohit and Major Manish led two squads each.

Shortly after he had seen his commandos off, Sen's cellphone rang. It was Major General Gupta. The IG had bad news. The police had told him that there were two militants inside the building. They had killed their hostages. Sen felt a tinge of regret. 'If only we had known earlier,' he thought to himself wistfully. The nature of the operation had changed from hostage rescue to seek and destroy. The NSG would attempt to kill the militants with no loss of their own.

Sen had established his fire base on the terrace of the six-storey Prem Bhawan directly behind Nariman House, from where his men had a commanding view of their objective. He stood on the roof with nine commandos, safety catches of their MP5s switched off, fingers on the triggers. Three of them carried AK-47s borrowed from the Mumbai police. Two 84 mm Carl Gustav rocket launchers sat at their feet. If the terrorists tried to fire on the helicopter, the RL would be fired into their hideout.

At 7.05 a.m., a grey IAF Mi-17 helicopter appeared, kicking up the clothes lines. It was an extremely short flight – the chopper had taken off from the *Kunjali* naval air station less than 500 metres away. A frisson of excitement coursed through Colaba market. The cloud of fear that had hung over the area for two days vanished. It was replaced by hype and insatiable curiosity. Sen could see TV cameras and journalists perched precariously on rooftops. There were hundreds of local residents too.

They lounged on water tanks and beneath cellphone towers. A curious resident even produced a pair of binoculars. Some relayed the news to friends on their cellphones, real time. They had ringside seats to the world's ultimate reality show.

'It's like they're watching a cricket match.' Sen shook his head in annoyance. A bullet from the terrorists could hit the people watching the spectacle. But a ring of snipers had kept the heads of the terrorists down. The NSG snipers checked their ammunition, cocked their rifles and peered down their Hensoldt-scopes, crosshairs firmly on the barred windows of the building. They waited for Sen's command to blast away at the windows.

From the roof of Batra House, the commandos saw the helicopter take off, clatter out into the sea over the harbour and then swing around back towards them. The clamshell cargo doors that opened out at the aircraft's rear had been detached even before it arrived in Mumbai the previous day. The NSG commandos now stood inside queued up on the sides. The pilot pointed its nose into the sea wind, lifted the collective, the lever that controlled the rotor speed, about two-thirds of the way up, pushed the right rudder pedal to nearly three-fourths of its full travel and tilted the cyclic (joystick) slightly to the right. The twelve-ton machine hovered over the building. The roar of the rotors had now turned into a distinctive chik-chik-chik sound.

An air force crewman threw out a single rope that had been tethered to a boom above the cargo rope. The commandos reached out with both hands for the rope and effortlessly slid down onto Nariman House. The drop zone was the terrace of the building, an area less than 150 square feet. It looked easy, but the operation was fraught with risk. A lattice of thin wires criss-crossed the buildings around Nariman House. These wires could snag the weighted rope. The Mi-17 was not the ideal platform for lowering commandos into built-up areas. Its rotors generated a tremendous prop wash which scattered debris, posing a threat to the aircraft itself. In less than a minute, twenty Black Cats had slithered down a weighted thirty-metre-long rope. Their boots thudded on the white-and-blue tiled roof, their MP5s at the ready.

They weren't the only ones watching. Back in the control room in Karachi, the LeT's handlers saw the helicopter atop Nariman House.

Handler: Heli aa gaya oopar?

Babar Imran: Humare oopar heli aa gaya hai.

Handler: Fire, fire, fire …

Babar Imran: Fire shuru ho gaya hai, fire shuru ho gaya hai … barabar se fire shuru ho gaya hai. Umar! Cover lo, cover lo.

Babar Imran: Humare kamre mein fire shuru ho gaya hai, humare kamre mein fire shuru ho gaya hai …

The live telecast of the operation put both the chopper and the commandos at risk. It revealed the number of troopers and the weapons they carried. A trained military hand knows what to see. The handlers in Pakistan dutifully relayed what they saw to the Nariman House attackers. They instructed the duo to assume 'cross positions' within the 300-square-foot living room. The terrorists knew what this meant. They moved sofas and refrigerators to form barricades at two ends of the room. They sat behind this. Only their rifle barrels poked out of these makeshift bunkers covering the door from both sides. The only entrance to the fourth floor was a deadly field of fire.

Major Manish led his commandos down to the building. They carefully descended in a single file down a fifteen-foot-long narrow metal ladder that led to the floor below. A commando reached for the single room on the terrace of the building. He tossed a flash bang grenade inside. It exploded with an orange crack. The commandos entered cautiously. The room was empty. Manish quickly took position. He shouted and tried to confirm the presence of civilians on the sixth floor. There was silence.

Swinging their MP5s in front, they walked down the door that led into the building. The green granite–coated staircase was narrow. Barely wide enough to allow two people to walk abreast. The commandos padded down noiselessly in a single file, two feet apart, slightly crouched. The black file entered the fifth floor. The door was slightly ajar. They tossed in another flash bang grenade and swiftly entered, their weapons covering all the corners. There was no one inside. The room was clear. It was a guest room.

Manish took out a white handkerchief and waved it in the window. A TV channel picked it up. 'Terrorists in Nariman House are surrendering,' one of the channels reported. Sen's phone rang. It was Major General Gupta. 'Who is surrendering,' he wanted to know. An exasperated Sen told him it was a prearranged signal. Snipers were poised on their perches around the building with their fingers on the trigger. Sen did not want them shooting their comrades.

The commandos descended to the fourth floor of the building. The wooden elevator door had been destroyed in the stairwell blast and hung limply over the shaft. The door to the flat was shut. There was silence. The commandos stood on one side and gently turned the steel-knobbed door lock. It was locked. Manish decided to blast it open. He called for the breacher, V. Satish, a sapper, who laid the explosive charges.

Captain Mohit stood with his squad mates, Havildar Hira Lal, Havildar Anthony Samy, Naib Subedar Rasool Mohammad and Havildar Ram Niwas, on the landing just above the flat as Satish walked down and placed a pole

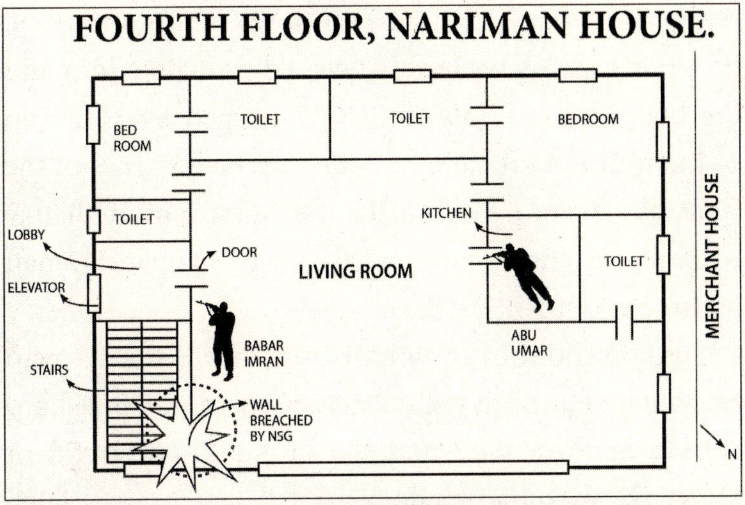

charge on the door. This was a five-foot-long bamboo stick packed with plastic explosives, ideal for smashing wooden doors. As the commandos moved back, Satish expertly drew an electrical wire attached to the pole and drew it up the flight of stairs. The commandos tensed themselves along the corridor, weapons at ready. Satish hooked the wire to a simple 12-volt battery that he pulled out of his pocket. In a micro-second, an electric current surged through the wire and into the detonator. A vertical section of the plywood door blew into the flat with a crackle.

Even before the smoke had settled, the commandos moved in. Gajender Singh Bisht charged down the stairs through the splintered door. An AK-47 opened up from inside. Crack! Crack! Crack! Bisht collapsed on the floor just outside the door. It was Abu Umar behind a small refrigerator that had been laid down across the floor, his body expertly wedged between the kitchen door and the living room. Only his AK-47 peeped over the top of the fridge. A grenade exploded in the confines of the stairwell. The noise was deafening. Manish immediately withdrew up the stairs. Hira Lal took cover inside a small bathroom outside the flat.

Sen, on the roof of Batra House, heard the staccato exchange of gunfire with concern. There was the sharp crackle of the AK-47 and the tat-tat-tat-tat sound of MP5s. His men had made contact. A few minutes later, Sen's walkie-talkie crackled. It was Major Manish. 'We've been hit. We've been hit. Commando down.'

In the melee of smoke, dust and gunfire, it wasn't clear who was hit, Gajender or Hira Lal. Mohit ran down the stairs to check. The commando was lying face down. A pool of blood spread around him on the green granite floor. Mohit saw the black running shoes. His heart sank. 'Gajender ...' Havildar Gajender's black dungaree-clad body lay motionless in what the NSG called the 'funnel of death', an area covered by the adversary's guns.

Just over an hour into the operation, and they had suffered a serious setback. Casualties were unacceptable in a seek-and-destroy mission. No one knew this better than Lt Col Sen. He slung his MP5 over his shoulder and scrambled down the stairs of Batra House. He saw a group of policemen sitting aimlessly at the foot of the building and lost his cool. 'What are you doing here?' he yelled at them. 'What if the terrorists get away?' The policemen sprang to their feet even as the officer dashed towards Merchant House like a man possessed.

Meanwhile, on the fourth floor of Nariman House, Major Manish, Captain Mohit and Ram Niwas fired at the unseen terrorists inside. Their low-velocity MP5 bullets could not penetrate the improvised pillboxes that the terrorists had set up. They also had to extricate Hira Lal – who stood in the terrorists' line of fire – from the small bathroom. Taking advantage of a lull in firing, Hira Lal sprinted up the stairs. A second grenade sailed out of the room and exploded near Mohit. 'Sahab! Grenade ...' Ram Niwas grabbed the officer by the collar and propelled him upstairs. The grenade exploded with an ear-splitting blast. It peppered their bodies with steel ball bearings. Slivers of pain shot up Mohit's leg. He limped up the stairs and towards the terrace.

Manish detailed Rasool Mohammad and Ram Niwas to cover the stairs and keep the militants pinned down. The rest of the team was reorganized. Mohit was left on the terrace under the care of Havildar Rajendra. The squads were redistributed between the terrace and fifth floor. The priority was to retrieve Gajender's body and the four grenades, an MP5 with five magazines and a pistol that he carried. Manish did not want the terrorists to replenish their arsenal.

As he clambered up the rooftop of Merchant House, the usually unflappable Sen shouted over his walkie-talkie. 'Save Gajender.' His concerns were different. He had seen the TV cameras that encircled Nariman House. What if the terrorists captured his commando alive? What if they strung his body outside Nariman House for the TV cameras? The thoughts raced through Sen's mind. 'All units, fire *karo*,' he shouted into his walkie-talkie. NSG men fired at Nariman House from three directions using AK-47s, MP5s and sniper rifles. 'They must not get him,' Sen shouted to his men.

The Merchant House terrace was crowned by a three-foot thick concrete crenellation with a false rose window in the centre. Sen and his support weapon squad now took shelter behind this. He took a Franchi Spas gun from the engineers. This Italian-made weapon resembles an assault rifle. It is a twelve-gauge semi-automatic shotgun that fired breaching rounds that can be placed just six inches away from door hinges and locks to blast them away. The gun also had tear gas rounds. Sen loaded six of them into the box magazine. He then aimed at the gap in the windows and fired one after the other. But the shells were ineffective. He needed something bigger. He pulled out the walkie-talkie clipped onto his left epaulette loop and hailed the operations centre. 'Bhandari, send me tear gas ... to the rooftop of Merchant House. Over.'

The fusillade of bullets from the commandos had

hit at least one of the terrorists. Now, he contacted his handler in Karachi, one last time.

Babar Imran: I've been shot, pray for me …

Handler: Kahaan laga hai, kahaan laga hai? Kahaan laga hai?

Babar Imran: One in my arm, one in my leg …

Handler: God protect you. Did you manage to kill them?

Babar Imran: We killed the commando who was entering … pray that God accepts my martyrdom …

Handler: Al Hamdullah … Al Hamdullah … may God keep you with him.

In a few minutes, an elderly, bespectacled police constable appeared on the roof of Merchant House, carrying an ancient tear gas gun, which resembled a sawn-off folding shotgun, and a square box that carried a dozen rounds. He explained the use of the tear gas gun. It was like a shotgun. Sen cracked the breech open and loaded the first round and aimed towards Nariman House. It didn't fire. Sen broke open the breech. The gun had no firing pin. The constable mumbled an apology and disappeared.

Then, an object flew onto the terrace of Merchant House between the commandos. It hit the cement floor with a dull thunk. '*O teri* …' the men swore, split and threw themselves to their sides, heads down. It sounded like a grenade. After five seconds, Sen looked up at the 'grenade'. It was a small packet of biscuits, tossed helpfully by one of the people on the buildings nearby. Sen was livid. 'Don't ever throw anything at us ...' he admonished them.

Meanwhile, the elderly police constable reappeared. He wore a grin of satisfaction. He had a working tear gas gun. Sen loaded up and began firing tear gas shells into Nariman House. There was a half-hour lull. A thick gas cloud filled the room. Sen stood on the ledge, peering in, trying to get a closer look. Suddenly, Imran Babar rushed to the window, his face covered with a water-soaked pillow case. Babar wielded an AK-47. Sen could see the whites of his eyes. He stood at least five feet away from the window, and blasted single shots with his rifle at his tormentor. Blue sparks ricocheted off the grille. Sen took cover, then got up to fire another tear gas round. The shell knocked the grille down. '*Laddoo lao*,' he shouted to his men. They returned with a box of Indian Army–issue HE 36 hand grenades. The HE 36 was a World War II vintage hand grenade, notoriously unreliable. Sen pulled the pin out of a grenade. He tossed it in like he would chuck a cricket ball. The grenade exploded inside with a piercing roar. In a little over thirty minutes, the officer threw in over a dozen hand grenades into the room – a series of deafening explosions rent the room. One of the grenades fell into the gap between the buildings. Fortunately, it did not explode.

This explosive distraction was what the commandos at the other end were waiting for. Havildar Ram Niwas threw a fire hook on Gajender's body. The commandos then gently pulled their comrade up the stairs. They felt his pulse. He was dead. His rifle plate had stopped a bullet, but he had been hit in the neck and left flank.

The troopers solemnly carried their fallen comrade's blood-soaked body to the terrace. He was placed inside the solitary room on the rooftop. They took a bed sheet from the room and covered his body. Gajender's MP5, with its NSG inventory number '279' hand-painted in white near the selector switch, was placed near his body.

The fourth floor had by now filled with tear gas smoke. The commandos could not see. Their eyes were red and watering, they coughed, their mouths ran dry and they felt nauseated. The men coughed and wheezed as they withdrew to the terrace.

'*Sahab*,' Hira Lal coughed and pointed at Mohit's leg, '*khoon nikal raha hai*.' Mohit rolled up the leg of his trouser. Grenade shrapnel had dug holes in his calf. Blood flowed down his leg. There was no field dressing kit in sight, so Mohit asked the engineers to throw him some black duct tape. He wrapped it around his leg.

A funereal gloom hung over the Black Cats who sat on the roof of Nariman House. Most had rolled their balaclavas over their heads like black funeral bands. These were men who had passed some of the toughest physical courses in the country. But that didn't inure them to the pain of losing a comrade. Gajender's body was mute testimony that perhaps they had failed him. The worst might yet be to come.

Mohit's cellphone rang. He pulled it out of the pocket of his dungaree. It was Keshar, his fiancée. He took the call. 'Mohit …' she said hesitantly, 'Sandeep is dead.' The news hit him like a bolt of lightning. He was shocked and speechless. He quietly asked Manish to accompany him to the fifth floor. The men could not be told of this – it was bad for morale. As he broke the news of Major Unnikrishnan's death, tears streamed down Mohit's cheeks: 'Sir, *inko nahin chhodoonga*. I'm going to get them.' Manish held his shoulders, looked at him straight in the eye and shook him. 'Mohit, *tu ulta kaam nahin karega* …'

Mohit was an engineer officer or 'sapper' on deputation. Commissioned into the Madras Engineer Group, he prided himself on having entered the NSG on a general duties vacancy after competing with infantry officers. Now, he would use his skills as a sapper. He switched his radio set off and thought fast. They needed a new entry into the flat. In his brief NSG stint, Mohit had made over 200 shaped charges. Varying quantities of plastic explosives designed to cut through airplane doors, concrete and machinery.

Manish asked if they could blow up the floor of the fifth floor, landing, quite literally, on top of the terrorists.

Mohit disagreed. Nariman House was a reinforced cement concrete (RCC) structure, he explained. If one slab collapsed, it might threaten the next one too. Then, Mohit looked at the walls. 'But the walls are made of bricks ...' The brick wall wasn't more than nine inches thick. A plan had begun taking shape. It was 4.30 p.m.

His cellphone rang again. It was Sen. 'Chhote, *tera* radio *kyon* off *hai?*' Sen asked, his voice calm, his tone avuncular.

'Sir,' Mohit began, 'Gajender is dead, and there's a lot of pressure on us.'

'Don't worry,' Sen counselled him. 'Gajender did what he had to do, now you do your duty.' Sen's voice masked his apprehensions. If the terrorists held off until sunset, Sen knew the siege would continue until next morning.

But now, Mohit had a plan. Sen listened and approved. At H-hour, the exact time at which Mohit would enter the fourth floor, Captain Kush Kashyap would lead the remaining commandos up Nariman House.

H-hour was fixed at 5 p.m. It took Mohit half an hour to shape a 2-kg slab of PEK. The plastic explosive was black and easily moulded, like a child's clay dough. He packed the clay into the hollow of a wooden 'door frame' that the NSG carried with them, and wrapped the gunny sacking around to hold the explosive in place. Mohit then plunged a pencil-sized detonator into it and drew the electrical wire from it. That done, he wiped his greasy hands on his dungarees and surveyed his handiwork. 'We're ready to rock,' he told Manish.

Sen, meanwhile, had decided to blow down the windows. If the house was dark, the commandos would have trouble adjusting when they broke inside. He climbed a two-storey tenement that overlooked Nariman House just 100 metres away. Two soldiers from the military unit in Colaba were posted there. One of them had his hands poised over an AGS-17 automatic grenade launcher (AGL). The AGL was kept on a metal table borrowed from a tenant of the building, its stubby barrel a little behind a two-foot-wide window cut in the concrete. A green drum magazine held twenty-nine grenades.

The troopers had placed sandbags around the AGL's metal legs to stabilize it. Sen directed the fire. He knew the soldiers had never fired a shot in the middle of a city; for that matter, neither had he. The grenadier curled his hands over the twin motorcycle-like handgrips, thumbs on the twin triggers at the back of the weapon. He peeped through the iron sights set slightly off to the left of the barrel and aimed the weapon at the orange curtains. The AGL jerked and reared on its forelegs like a horse before it belched out six rounds. A few shells crashed into the concrete just below the fourth-floor window and exploded, others hit the grilles. The curtains were destroyed, the window frame burst and hung limply over the building. Sunlight streamed into the shattered building. Snipers now had a clear field of fire.

As the grenade shells thudded into the building, Mohit stood up and asked for a volunteer. The explosive would breach the wall, creating a gap for just two people to enter. Any more and the men risked taking casualties. 'Who will go with me?' he looked around the troopers. A hand shot up. It was Lance Naik V. Satish, one of the two sapper commandos in the group. 'Sahab, take an infantryman or a para-SF guy along,' one of the NSG commandos suggested. Satish seethed at the suggestion, but didn't react. He was determined to go. However, the Spas shotgun he had was useless in a firefight. He needed a weapon. Troopers are usually reluctant to part with their personal weapons. Satish knew what he had to do. He calmly walked over to Gajender's body, bent down to pick up his MP5, inserted a clip into it and cocked the weapon. 'Let's go sir.' The two men headed back into the building, carrying the shaped charge.

At 5 p.m., a thunderous explosion shook Nariman House. The door frame charge punched a three-foot-wide hole into the wall of the fourth floor. The pressure wave from the back blast simultaneously slammed an identical hole in the outer wall of the building, throwing debris on the red-tiled roof of the three-storeyed Abdulbhai Karimji building next to it. Thick white smoke and reddish-brown brick dust covered the stairwell.

Satish leapt into the breach. Mohit followed. Manish covered the door. Imran Babar was sitting against the wall. He had been stunned by the force of the blast. His face was covered by red and grey brick and plaster dust. But he had levelled his AK-47 at the yawning gap. He saw Satish's black-dungareed figure leap into the hazy room. Babar stood up from behind the sofa, ghost-like. Satish was barely five feet away from him. Babar fired. And missed. Satish turned around in a split second and fired a series of single shots. He did not miss. Babar collapsed and fell backwards. The AK-47 dropped from his lifeless hands.

The inert body of Abu Umar lay across the room, his right leg folded under his body. He had fallen backwards, violently twisted, his torso severely burnt. Both terrorists sported the red 'kalava' threads Headley had bought for them.

The commandos quickly entered the room. They kicked the AK-47s away from the bodies of the two lifeless terrorists and headed inside. It was a slaughter house.

They saw the bodies of the two hostages on a bed inside the fourth floor. Rivka Holtzberg and Norma Shvarzblat-Rabinovich lay where they had been executed, bound and blindfolded with strips of cloth. Their faces and bodies were mutilated. The bodies of Rabbi Gavriel Holtzberg, Yocheved Orpaz and Bentzion Chroman were on the second floor. In the small library lay the body of Rabbi Leibisch Teitelbaum, bloated and face down in a pile of black ooze. He had been shot in front of the bookshelves filled with leather-bound Jewish texts.

When the restive crowds outside heard the explosion, there was a mad stampede towards Nariman House. The crowds surged forward and swamped the police units and later the army units who had cordoned off the house. The match had ended. The fans were swamping the cricket ground.

A policeman ran frantically to Lt Col Sen. 'Sir, please fire.' Sen didn't understand.

The police officer was desperate. 'Please help us. Please fire, or there will be a stampede.'

Sen cocked his head sideways and spoke into his walkie-talkie. 'Throw a stun grenade.' An officer complied. A muffled blast was heard through the house. The crowds stood back, a trifle confused. Perhaps, the operations were still on. They held back.

Sen allowed himself a smile. His probationers had passed their test.

Aftermath

Prime Minister's Office, South Block, 28 November 2008, 6 p.m.
The top brass of the three armed forces and the chiefs of India's intelligence services filed past the spotlessly clean sandstone corridors and turned into the conference room at the far end of the corridor. After entering, they sat down around the long table at the centre of the room. The men were grim. The usual banter was missing. Few made eye contact with each other, looking at the room décor instead. The two giant TV screens on both walls of the wood-panelled room were blank. It was a brief respite from the nearly forty hours of non-stop television footage of a city under siege.

By then, the pieces of the puzzle had begun falling in place. There was no doubt that the attackers had come from Pakistan. One terrorist Ajmal Kasab, captured alive by a heroic Mumbai policeman, had unravelled the conspiracy to cause mayhem and kill as many civilians as possible. The Intelligence Bureau had intercepted conversations between the Pakistan-based handlers and the terrorists even as the attacks were on. Five terrorists had been killed so far and the remaining four were holed up in the north wing of the Taj Palace fighting off the NSG.

National Security Adviser M.K. Narayanan sat at the head of the long table. But not for long. Prime Minister Manmohan Singh walked in ten minutes later and took his place. The PM had been mulling over the question that had bedevilled his predecessors from Narasimha Rao to Atal Bihari Vajpayee – India's options in case of a covert cross-border thrust from Pakistan. 'What is it that you all can do,' he asked the grim faces around the table.

There were few options. Navy chief Admiral Sureesh Mehta said that his force was not ready for war. 'We have nothing like Cold Start,' he said, alluding to the army doctrine that called for swift retaliation against Pakistan in case of a grave provocation. Vice Chief of Army Staff, Lt General Milan Naidu, standing in for Army Chief General Deepak Kapoor who was away on a tour of South Africa, said he would rather wait for the army chief to return. Air Force Chief Air Chief Marshal Fali Homi Major sounded the only positive note. 'Give me a clear list of targets and I can mount air strikes in sixteen hours,' he said. The meeting was inconclusive.

Prime Minister's Office, South Block, 4 December 2008, 5.30 p.m.

Admiral Sureesh Mehta told a press conference on 2 December 2008 that the intelligence alerts the navy received on 19 November (the coordinates of the LeT vessel) were 'not actionable' and that there was a 'systemic failure' which had to be taken stock of.

The full extent of this systemic failure was revealed two days later when India's security establishment met again at the prime minister's office. India, it was revealed, lacked the intelligence, capability or the political will to retaliate if there was a major terrorist attack. A key recommendation of a group of ministers set up after the Kargil War, that leaders of the military, executive and legislature indulge in regular politico-military war gaming, had never been implemented.

It was exactly a week after the terrorists had landed on Mumbai's shores and the dead and injured in the attacks had been counted. The initial shock of the attack had worn off, giving way to outrage. The government had already ruled out a full-scale mobilization of the armed forces like the one after the 13 December 2001 terrorist attack on India's parliament.

The three service chiefs, the heads of the IB and R&AW now gathered around the PM to discuss other options to respond. The prime minister turned to Army Chief General Deepak Kapoor: 'Did the army have a plan to punish Pakistan?'

'Before I answer this question, I should ask whether the nation is prepared to pay the price for it...' General Deepak Kapoor began. He was interrupted by Defence Minister A.K. Antony: 'Chief, we will worry about the nation...you just answer the question...'

Both the army and navy, it emerged in the meeting, were unprepared. The only person who did seem prepared with options that evening was National Security Adviser M.K. Narayanan. The NSA, a veteran who had headed the Intelligence Bureau, now presented five alternatives. Each had an implication and an escalation dynamic or the possible consequences each would result in.

The first was a covert option of targeting Lashkar-e-Taiba leadership. The second, limited air strikes against terrorist training camps in Pakistan-occupied Kashmir (PoK). The third, a limited war confined to J&K, with full mobilization of the army to ensure Pakistan could not deploy its reserves against the point of attack. The fourth, air strikes by the IAF backed up by partial mobilization of the army. The fifth, a helicopter gunship raid by Indian army special forces against terrorist camps and launch pads across the border.

But as Narayanan discovered, the options were ambitious beyond the range and capabilities of either the armed forces or the intelligence agencies. Each option was successively discarded. Despite two decades of a covert war waged from across the border, neither the army nor intelligence agencies had assets on the ground. Another factor complicating a military response was the presence of the US military at a number of airbases on Pakistani soil as part of Operation Enduring Freedom in Afghanistan. This meant an Indian response would have to be confined to Pakistan Occupied Kashmir (PoK) where a majority of LeT training camps were. A heliborne raid required fighter aircraft to carry out supression of enemy air defences (SEAD) in the target area, an aerial escort package of fighter aircraft and pinpoint last- minute intelligence on the presence inside the target camp. This alternative was rejected. The possibility of an escalation of a war limited to Jammu and Kashmir was also discussed but set aside. India lacked the margin of conventional superiority over Pakistan that would allow it to dominate and control the escalation ladder.

The option that sounded the most logical with a controllable outcome was the option to strike at terrorist training camps in PoK which the Air Chief Major had rooted for in the first meeting. 'We have the capability to lob a laser-guided bomb across the border,' Air Chief Marshal Major said, 'but somebody has to be there to lase the target.' The option was a non-starter. R&AW confessed they did not have assets on the ground who could illuminate the target for jet strikes. Moreover, the camps were temporary and located near civilian areas.

Destroying them could result in collateral damage. Talk of hard options against Pakistan was discarded. It was now left to the diplomats to take over and mount global pressure on Pakistan.

Epilogue

In June 2014, Mohammed Naveed Jutt, a Pakistani terrorist from Multan, who was arrested from south Kashmir, made an interesting revelation. He told his interrogators from the Jammu and Kashmir police of how LeT instructors at the Maskar Aksa training camp in Pakistan Occupied Kashmir cautioned recruits against repeating Ajmal Kasab's mistakes. These included a failure to sink the MFV *Kuber*, destroy a satellite phone, and, finally, compromising the entire operation by being captured alive.

What would the aftermath have looked like had Kasab and his comrades in mayhem followed their instructions to a T? The *Kuber*, and its hapless captain Solanki, would have silently dissolved into the Arabian Sea floor off Mumbai. The Mumbai police would have been left with an inflatable boat, ten unidentified bodies from four bloody sieges including one at the CST station building. A host of red herrings – red threads and student ID cards from colleges in Hyderabad, and the reference to a

'Deccan Mujahideen' would spawn conspiracy theories of the attackers being dissatisfied Indian youth.

But, fortuitously, the enormous electronic and material footprint left behind by the perpetrators, averted what the spy world calls, a 'plausible deniable operation'. The testimony of the sole surviving terrorist Ajmal Kasab, from Okara village in Faridkot, Pakistani Punjab (executed in Pune in November 2012), and accounts from the LeT scout David Coleman Headley and Abu Jundal, an Indian who motivated the attackers from a Karachi control room, have since peeled away the complex, multi-layered 26/11 plot. The weight of the evidence conclusively indicate Pakistani support, even sponsorship, of the attacks.

Most of their leads end at the grey headquarters of the Inter Services Intelligence Directorate, or ISI, on Islamabad's Khayaban-e-Suhrawardy avenue. Predictably, ISI officials who briefed foreign journalists in 2009 insinuated the attacks were staged by Indian officials to cover up a probe into attacks by Hindu extremists. On 25 November 2009, Pakistan's Federal Investigative Agency (FIA) chargesheeted seven prime accused for the 26/11 attacks. They included Zaki-ur-Rahman Lakhvi, Hammad Amin Sadiq, Mazhar Iqbal alias Abu al-Qama, Abdul Wajid alias Zarrar Shah, Shahid Jamil Riaz, Jamil Ahmad and Younas Anjum – and twenty others who set up training camps at Yousuf

Goth in Karachi and Mirpur Sakro in Thatta in Sindh province and obtained firearms, grenades and explosives for carrying out the attacks.

Five years later, however, the trial drags on. As of September 2014, seven hearings of the case in Pakistan's anti-terrorism court in Rawalpindi had been postponed. Very clearly it had to do with the spectre of death that haunts prosecutors. On 3 May 2013, Chaudhry Zulfiqar Ali, chief prosecutor in the 26/11 case who promised 'to leave no stone unturned to bring the perpetrators to justice' was gunned down in Islamabad. LeT supremo Hafiz Mohammed Saeed, who Kasab said saw off the ten terrorists as they sailed out of Karachi, continues to roam free in Pakistan. The LeT's military commander Lakhvi continues to direct operations and fund raising activities from within Lahore's high security Adiala jail.

Pakistan, has refused to hand over voice samples of Lakhvi and other LeT plotters which could be matched with the telephone intercepts of the 26/11 controllers. Islamabad's inactivity is the latest in a long line of unresolved issues between the two countries including the 1993 Mumbai blasts and the 1999 hijacking of Indian Airlines Flight IC 814 to Afghanistan. Pakistan's official line, that more evidence is needed to convict the 26/11 plotters, has failed to cut ice. Responding to one such statement by the Pakistan Foreign Office statement, India's foreign ministry spokesperson Syed Akbaruddin said this on 26 October 2013:

> The entire planning of the dastardly Mumbai terrorist attack was hatched in Pakistan, the training of the terrorists who launched that attack was undertaken in Pakistan, the financing of the conspiracy was in Pakistan. It, therefore, follows that 99 per cent of the evidence will be available in Pakistan. It is incumbent on the authorities there to present that evidence in order to bring to book the perpetrators of the Mumbai attacks.

The Narendra Modi government lodged India's diplomatic protests over the slow-moving trial with Islamabad two months after it was sworn in on May 26 this year. As Gujarat Chief Minister, Modi grasped the changed dimensions of the 26/11 attacks and its global dimension. 'This is for the first time Pakistan has allowed use of sea routes to further terrorism against India,' he said at the Oberoi-Trident hotel on 28 November as the hotels were being cleared by security forces. 'Terrorists have targeted US, British and Israeli citizens.'

His government now has to deal with Prime Minister Nawaz Sharif, sworn into office in June 2013 after Pakistan's first ever electoral transition. The Sharif government has shown little inclination to comply with a list of Indian demands: hand over the 26/11 conspirators to India, extradite previous conspirators like Dawood Ibrahim or dismantle the infrastructure of terrorism. Pakistan's political leadership lives in the shadow of the army that controls foreign policy as firmly as it does the world's fastest-growing nuclear arsenal and a covert force of non-state actors.

'It's like that old story,' US Secretary of State Hilary Clinton said at a press conference in Islamabad on October 2011, 'you can't keep snakes in your backyard and expect them only to bite your neighbours. Eventually those snakes are going to turn on whoever has them in the backyard,' to convey dismay over Pakistan sheltering insurgent groups to destabilize Afghanistan.

The Pakistan army's bewildering array of poisonous snakes includes the LeT and also Sikh separatist leaders like Wadhwa Singh and Paramjit Singh Panjwar. This, even as the army battles what its 2012 assessment called an internal security situation that presents its gravest risk to its existence. Since 2007, the deadly Tehrik-i-Taliban Pakistan (TTP), has unleashed a wave of suicide attacks on airports, military installations and cities, forcing the army to attack TTP sanctuaries in North Waziristan.

The departure of the US and NATO forces from Afghanistan in late 2014, and the removal of its panoply of surveillance capabilities, will have the effect of, in the words of one Indian intelligence official, 'turning the lights off in a nuclear-armed sub-continent'. It will add another element of dramatic uncertainty in a region crawling with non-state actors and ambitious armies. Indian leaders are clear that future attacks will not go unpunished. Speaking at the *India Today* conclave on 12 March 2012, the then home minister P Chidambaram ruled out war as an option against Pakistan but said, 'If it is reasonably established that any 26/11 type attack in future has its origin in Pakistan, India's response will be swift and decisive.'

But what of the lessons learned from the attacks? The Kargil war between India and Pakistan in the summer of 1999 prompted the setting up of the Kargil Review Committee headed by defence expert K Subrahmanyam in 2001, the first ever such publicly disseminated inquiry. The 26/11 attacks led to the constitution of a High-Level Inquiry Committee headed by former home secretary Ram Pradhan and including IPS officer V Balachandran. The two-member committee submitted a ninety-page report to the Maharashtra government, making the attacks seem a localized event. The two-member state inquiry committee had no jurisdiction over the Central forces. A comprehensive inquiry would have established, for instance, why a battle-hardened army battalion, based just two kilometres away, was used only as a perimeter-guarding force; why the crisis management team of the Central government did not meet until a day after the attacks; why the 51 SAG took nearly twelve hours to arrive from Delhi when a fly-away team of 150 commandos was kept on round-the-clock alert with an aircraft. Why the Indian Navy and the Coast Guard did not respond to intelligence alerts and failed to prevent the attacks, just as the army missed the stealthy insertion of an entire Pakistani brigade disguised as infiltrators, on the Kargil heights in 1999.

The NSG's 51 SAG found itself tested by the first-ever use of multiple sieges, and commendably handled what was a nightmare scenario for any counter-terrorist force. But its forty-three-page internal after-action report does not appear comprehensive enough for any serious understanding of the operation.

What did happen, in the aftermath, however, were spurts of hardware procurement and expansion of forces. The Mumbai police 'Force One' SWAT team raised a year after the attacks equipped itself with a dazzling array of firearms but has had inadequate firing practice. Weapons alone may not be the solution. Just two of the terrorists who rampaged through CST station and on the streets outside on the night of November 26, accounted for nearly a third of the 166 fatalities in the attack. Just one well trained policeman with a functioning bolt-action rifle could have averted this catastrophe. The police force, the first responders to a crisis, still suffer enormous deficiencies in manpower and training, facts noted by successive police reform commissions. India has just 134 policemen per 100,000 people. The US and the United Kingdom have ratios of 248 and 301 policemen respectively for similar number of people. Procurements continue at a slow, bureaucratic pace. In July 2014, the Maharashtra government invited tenders to install 5,000 Close Circuit TV Cameras at vital locations all over the city, the fourth time such tenders were called for in six years.

The attacks were not novel as far as fighting in built-up areas was concerned. These have been a constant feature of most counter-terrorist operations since the 1970s. The real challenges were those of command and control and mobilization of resources to deal with a multi-site attack. The marine commandos, for instance, were inducted early on only because a senior bureaucrat learned of their existence from a friend. European Union countries are believed to be working on pan-European level tactical cooperation in such a crisis. Several global police forces and SWAT team sent in their operators into Mumbai to learn how to counter such attacks and have even rehearsed responses to such scenarios. The Delhi-based Bureau of Police Research and Development is believed to have put together a manual on the response to such a crisis, but till date, there is no evidence that it has been rehearsed in any Indian city.

The home ministry's Multi-Agency Centre (MAC), an Intelligence Bureau-manned forum, now sees representatives of all India's twenty-three Central intelligence agencies meeting every day to pool leads. The MAC, however, suffers from a shortage of trained analysts who could join the dots on emerging threats. The NSG has doubled in size to over 12,000 personnel to man hubs set up in Kolkata, Ahmedabad, Hyderabad, Chennai and Mumbai to provide a quicker response to Mumbai-like attacks. This dispersal does not, however, address its fundamental flaw, the lack of a permanent core. The force is staffed by personnel on deputation and remains severely constrained by lack of proper equipment and training.

The NSG's counter-terrorist wing, the 51 SAG, and its counter-hijack wing, the 52 SAG, are staffed by personnel loaned by the army. A specialist ethos, it can be argued, cannot be driven without a permanent structure and longer tenures. A proposal made by its founders nearly three decades ago for a permanent 25 per cent staff component has still not been implemented. This has resulted in an organization which is a curious hybrid of police, paramilitary and army whose standard black fatigues barely disguise internal contradictions. All the 51 SAG veterans who saw action in 26/11 are gone, their unique experience subsumed in the ocean of the Indian army.

When it comes to procurements, the NSG's contradictions turned into a three-legged race that also included the home ministry's civilian bureaucrats. The force trains in isolation, without manuals and with little improvements on drills handed down from one training officer to another for over two decades.

The SAG's three critical support arms have atrophied. The Electronic Support Group cannot intercept communications or set up a mobile command post to guide operations, the Technical Support Group lacks equipment to snoop in on terrorists and the Support Weapons Squadron is still bereft of specialized equipment to swiftly breach targets. Bafflingly, it does not even have basic equipment like armoured shields that could save lives of troopers storming defended rooms.

The NSG's high point each year continues to be the annual raising day celebration every 17 October at their sports stadium in Manesar, Haryana, which claims money, time and effort. Commandos storm garish Bollywood movie sets, shoot clay pots filled with colored water before cheering home ministry officials, their families and the media.

The Special Ranger Group, staffed with volunteers drawn from home ministry forces, usually travelled with the SAG. In this instance, they had been taken away by the home ministry to guard India's growing number of VVIPs. Black dungaree clad commandos continue to be a politician's most sought after status symbol. One chief minister shooed her police guards away and directed she be flanked by her NSG commandos for a magazine cover shoot.

The Indian army's plan to equip all its 'ghatak platoons', a commando unit in all infantry units with SWAT tools – door breaching grenades and sub-machine guns – for Mumbai-type operations, is stuck in a bureaucratic maze. The Indian Navy now polices the brown waters off the Indian coast, buying small patrol craft and raising defensive forces Naval brass worry about the impact of such deployments on their blue water ambitions.

Most of the NSG's 51 SAG officers and men continue to serve in the Indian Army. Some with medals, others with memories of those fateful 48 hours in Mumbai. Major Sandeep Unnikrishnan and Havildar Gajender Singh were posthumously decorated with the Ashok Chakra, India's highest peacetime gallantry award. (Also posthumously awarded to Mumbai police officers Hemant Karkare, Ashok Kamte, Vijay Salaskar and Tukaram Omble.)

Lance Naik V. Satish was awarded the Kirti Chakra; Captain A.K. Singh and Naik P.V. Manesh were decorated with Shaurya Chakras. Major Sanjay Kandwal, Major Manish Mehrotra and Major Saurabh Shah were decorated with Sena Medals, for 'exceptional duty and courage'. Captain Mohit Dhingra was given an NSG

Director General's commendation card and now sports a tattoo on his chest, just above his heart: Unni.

'Mumbai-style attacks will inevitably be repeated. Terrorist groups and their state sponsors have been quick to realize the benefits of such high-visibility strikes. Four al-Shabaab gunmen carried out a Mumbai-style attack during the September 2013 four-day siege of the Westgate Shopping Mall in Nairobi, Kenya in which seventy-two civilians were killed. At a time when insurgent groups like the Islamic State of Iraq and Al Sham (ISIS) have demonstrated their ability to capture and hold territory from states and are attracting global recruits, swarm attacks like those in Mumbai could prove to be their weapon of choice to inflict terror. The Mumbai attacks were a monumental tragedy. The failure to learn from it will be a bigger one yet.

Ten Years Later

The hybrid attacks of 26/11 were almost certainly the inspiration behind the 13 November 2015 attacks on Paris by seven ISIS suicide attackers that killed 130 persons.

As pointed out by this book in 2014, the Mumbai attacks offered a copybook example for non-state actors on how to paralyse a global metropolis by simultaneously striking at multiple civilian targets. But this is clearly where the similarities between ISIS and the LeT end.

By December 2017 a global coalition had defeated ISIS and driven them out from the territory it controlled most in Syria and Iraq. In sharp constrast, the LeT continues to operate with impunity inside Pakistan, suggesting just how blurred the lines between the state and non-state are in this part of the world.

'Militant organizations are active,' Pakistan's former PM Nawaz Sharif said in an interview to the Karachi-based *Dawn* newspaper published on 12 May 2018. 'Call them non-state actors, should we allow them to cross the border and kill 150 people in Mumbai? Explain it to me. Why can't we complete the trial?' Sharif asked.

This is a question New Delhi has asked for over a decade and not received a satisfactory reply. LeT chief Hafiz Saeed was released from house-arrest in November 2017, on the ninth anniversary of the attacks and his party, the Allah-u-Akbar Tehreek (AAT), contested the country's 25 July 2018 general elections. The AAT predictably drew a blank in an election where Imran Khan's Pakistan Tehreek-i-Insaf (PTI) emerged as the single largest party yet, Saeed's political foray signalled a mainstreaming of his jihadi groups inside Pakistan. This, even as the trial of the 26/11 accused in Pakistan has dragged on in an Anti-Terrorist Court since 2009, is unusual for the special courts are meant to speedily decide trials.

The 1993 serial bombings, the 2006 train bombings and 26/11 – three major attacks over the span of fifteen years – revealed the Pakistani deep state's maniacal obsession with targeting India's economic capital through mass-casualty civilian attacks.

The slow-paced 26/11 trial continues to be one of the biggest stumbling blocks in the normalization of ties between the two countries even as newer attacks by Pakistan-based terrorists since 2015 brought the two countries on the precipice.

India's military planners believe there has been a subtle recalibration of Pakistan's twin strategic assets, nuclear weapons and non-state actors in the seven-year break between 26/11 and the resumption of suicide attacks in 2015. The shield of threats to use nuclear weapons are thought to have played their role in deterring an Indian military response to terror strikes. The most recent example of this was during Operation Parakram, the ten-month deployment of the Indian army after the 13 December 2001 attack on India's parliament by five Jaish-e-Mohammed (JeM) terrorists.

Post 26/11, Indian army planners see minor tweaks to this gameplan. The sword now only strikes at 'legitimate' military targets. The Pakistani nuclear deterrent has been refined with tactical nuclear weapons aimed at possible retaliation from the Indian army's Cold Start military doctrine. Cold Start evolved after the slow month-long mobilization of Parakram. It aims at swift and shallow punitive thrusts into Pakistan within forty-eight hours and well below the threshhold of nuclear weapon release.

The most significant part of the Pakistan army's counter Cold Start, Indian planners believe, unfolded with the April 2011 test-firing of the Nasr short-range ballistic missile. Pakistan, in an unambigously worded statement after the launch, claimed the Nasr 'added deterrence value to its strategic weapon's programme at short ranges'. Its 'nuclear warheads of appropriate yield with high accuracy' offered a 'quick response system' that addressed the need to 'deter evolving threats'.

The LeT attempts to evade global sanctions by morphing into the Jamaat ud-Dawah and later, the Falah-e-Insaniat Foundation have failed. The JuD and the FIF was added to the list of global terrorist organizations in 2008 and 2010 respectively and key LeT personnel including Hafiz Saeed were labelled 'Specially Designated Global Terrorists' with a $10 million bounty put out for Saeed's arrest.

The Pakistani deep state's response was to bring its other significant non-state actor out of the doghouse. Maulana Masood Azhar, head of the Jaish-e-Mohammed (JeM), out of favour with the Pervez Musharraf government for his group's involvement in an assassination attempt against President Pervez Musharraf in 2003, announced his group's return into GHQ Rawalpindi's good books with a massive rally in Muzaffarabad in PoK on 26 January 2014. In his first public rally, which he addressed over a telephone hooked to a public address system, Azhar called for war against India. 'Let us aim guns at India first,' he said. 'We will move to Israel and United States later,' his voice reverberated over speakers placed around the venue, ringed by dozens of the JeM's black-and-white flags and hundreds of his supporters.

Azhar's JeM, which he set up after being freed in exchange for the hijacked passengers of IC-814 in 1999, had earlier carried out the sensational strike on India's Parliament. The JeM had, since 2013, marked the return of fidayeen attacks in J&K after a three-year gap with deadly attacks on police stations, army camps and military convoys. In December 2014, they attacked an army camp in Uri, killing fourteen security personnel including a Lt Colonel. By 2015, they began striking outside J&K as well. The terror strike on a police station in Gurdaspur district by four JeM infiltrators on 25 July 2015, Punjab's first terror attack in over a decade, signalled that the organization was willing to take the fight into India's hinterland. In September 2016 four JeM terrorists tested the resolve of the Modi government with another sensational attack on an army unit in Uri which killed nineteen soldiers. India's response was to launch cross-border raids using special forces commandos crossing the Line of Control on foot to strike at Pakistani military posts at four locations. The 'surgical strikes', as the government called them, were carried out along a 100-kilometre front and monitored in real time by the army headquarters in New Delhi by the political executive and military top brass. The coordinated attacks at three camps where terrorists were believed to be sheltered before infiltration led to an undetermined number of casualties on the Pakistani side. The strikes were followed up by a statement read out by the Indian Army's Director General Military Operations which said that the Indian Army had conducted 'surgical strikes at several launch pads to pre-empt infiltration by terrorists'.

The DGMO said that the operations had caused 'significant casaulties' among the terrorists. The statement was politico-military signalling of the highest order. Mass-casualty terror strikes would not go unpunished.

The year 2015 marked the entry of another major player into Pakistan: the People's Republic of China. Chinese President Xi Jingping's visit to Islamabad flagged off the China–Pakistan Economic Corridor, a $62 billion network of infrastructure and special economic zones stretching from Xinjiang in south-western China to Gwadar in Balochistan. The Pakistan army sees in the CPEC a project that can graft a backbone into Pakistan's flailing economy and tighten the fraternal embrace between the two countries. One of the fringe benefits of this relationship has been China repeatedly blocking India's attempts to get the UN Security Council to list JeM chief Azhar as a global terrorist through 2017 and 2018.

The strategic partnership between India and the United States continues to be leavened by shared concerns on terrorism and the rise of China. The Trump administration which in Afghanistan has inherited the longest war in US history, sees Pakistan as being part of the problem and has slashed its funding by 75 per cent, from $1 billion to just 150 million this year.

The US action was a follow up to President Trump's New Year's day tweet decrying Pakistan's 'lies and deceit' in exchange for US aid and giving 'safe haven to the terrorists we hunt in Afghanistan'. Pakistan's troubles seemed to mount in February 2018, when the Financial Action Task Force (FATF) on money laundering, an initiative of G-7 member nations, placed it on the grey list for failing to curb terror funding. This move further complicates matters for the country's twenty-second Prime Minister, Imran Khan, sworn in on August 2018 on the promise of a 'Naya Pakistan'. The new Pakistan he promised has so far remained a mirage, teetering on the edge of financial bankruptcy, infested with militant groups in the north and south and with the military still firmly in the driver's seat.

Khan, widely perceived as a GHQ favourite, visited the headquarters of the ISI in September 2018 and called them Pakistan's 'first line of defence' and the 'world's best intelligence agency'.

On 6 September 2018, Foreign Minister Sushma Swaraj, Defence Minister Nirmala Sitharaman met their counterparts Secretary of State Mike Pompeo and Defence Secretary James Mattis New Delhi for their first annual 'Two Plus Two' dialogue. Both sides devoted significant portions of a three-page joint statement released at the culimination of their dialogue. Welcoming the expansion of a bilateral counter-terrorism cooperation, they reaffirmed their support for a UN Comprehensive Convention on International Terrorism that will advance and strengthen the framework for global cooperation and reinforce the message that no cause or grievance justifies terrorism. The ministers denounced the use of terrorist proxies in the region and called on Pakistan to ensure that the territory under its control is not used to launch terrorist attacks on other countries. On the eve of the tenth anniversary of the 26/11 Mumbai attack, they called on Pakistan to bring to justice expeditiously the perpetrators of the Mumbai, Pathankot, Uri and other cross-border terrorist attacks. So far, there has been no sign of compliance. On 12 September 2018, the Pakistani Supreme Court permitted the Jamaat-ud-Dawa (JuD) and its front organization, the Falahi Insaniyat Foundation (FIF) to continue their relief and charity work in the country, overturning a 1 January government order that year banning companies and individuals from making donations to the JuD, FIF and other organizations banned by the UN.

The government of India, meanwhile kept up its global diplomatic offensive against Pakistan, a country which they hinted hosts 132 UN designated terrorists and patronises twenty-two entities sanctioned under

UN Security Council 1267 and 1988 resolution regimes.

In her speech at the UN General Assembly on 29 September Foreign Minister Sushma Swaraj recalled the 11 September 2001 attacks whose mastermind Osama bin Laden had been killed by US Special Forces in the Pakistani garrison town of Abbotabad in 2011. 'Pakistan's commitment to terrorism as an instrument of official policy has not abated one bit,' Swaraj said. 'Neither has its belief in hypocrisy. The killers of 9/11 met their fate but the mastermind of 26/11, Hafiz Saeed, still roams the streets of Pakistan with impunity.'

suicide bomber killed forty CRPF troopers. In retaliation, IAF warplanes bombed a JeM terrorist training camp in Balakot, Khyber Pakhtunkhwa province less than a fortnight later, on 26 February, killing an undetermined number of terrorists. It was the first time IAF jets had crossed the international border since the 1971 war with Pakistan. With this the Narendra Modi government signalled its resolve to use its military might to tackle cross-border terrorism. A brief air duel between IAF and PAF (Pakistan Air Force) jets the following day saw an Indian jet downed and a pilot, Wing Commander Abhinandan Varthaman, taken prisoner. Pakistan returned him back to India within forty-eight hours, de-escalating the standoff.

India and Pakistan ties plunged to their lowest point since 26/11 just six months later when the Modi government announced on 5 August 2019 its decision to abrogate Article 370 in Jammu and Kashmir and divide the state into two union territories.

The possibility of further strikes by the Pakistani deep state's 'non-state actors' remains as high as ever. Only this time, the risk of their attack spilling into a major conventional war between the two countries is greater than it was in 2019.

Acknowledgements

This book began as a magazine article in a coffee shop in Connaught Place, New Delhi, some years ago. A National Security Guard officer, who is still in service and hence would like to remain anonymous, gave me a peep into Operation Black Tornado. When he had finished, I was clear the story of this unusual operation extended beyond the confines of a magazine article. That vision could not be realized without the Indian Army's Additional Directorate General of Public Information particularly Lieutenant General S.L. Narasimhan, Brigadier Sandeep Thapar and Brigadier Hitten Sahni and Captain PVS Satish, public relations officer, Indian Navy. My deepest gratitude to them for setting up the interviews with service personnel. It was also thanks to them that I met a set of remarkable individuals in uniform, the MARCOS and the officers and men of the 51 SAG. Dan Reed's superb 2009 documentary, 'Terror in Mumbai', for a clinically precise account of the attacks.

Some other friends helped complete the narrative. My friend from the coffee shop remained a sentient presence all through its writing. Another, 'Romeo Lima', offered me a hands-on introduction into the world of the 51 SAG, warts and all. My friend Captain Aarunikant Sinha (retired), who set up the first book meeting, joined me in monsoon drives through Mumbai as we met some of the key people in the story. I am thankful to all of you and value your guidance and friendship.

Agents 'A' and 'K', I am indebted for your time and insightful deep backgrounders; 'Lone Wolf', an island of uncompromising excellence in a rigid establishment, may your tribe increase.

Special thanks to V.K. Karthika, chief editor and publisher at HarperCollins India, for seeing a book in the bare bones of an idea.

Thanks are due to my former colleague and *Accidental India* author Shankkar Aiyar for never being more than a phone call away. My friend Brigadier Xerxes Adrianwalla (retired), for his critical inputs; Brigadier Govind Singh Sisodia (retired), the man in the centre of the Tornado, for his unique insights into the operation.

Several other officials helped fill the run-up to the deployment of the NSG. Former cabinet secretary K.M. Chandrasekhar, Maharashtra state chief secretary Johny Joseph, Special Secretary (Internal Security) M.L. Kumawat, former DG NSG J.K. Dutt, IG (Ops) Major

General Abhay Gupta, former secretary ARC Sanjeev Tripathi and Colonel Arun Sharma, former commanding officer of the 2 Grenadiers and former special secretary, cabinet secretariat, Vappala Balachandran. I am grateful to all of you.

I would also like to thank colleagues at my workplace *India Today*. My editor-in-chief Aroon Purie who has been inspirational part of my professional life for fourteen years. My former editorial director M.J. Akbar; my editor Kaveree Bamzai for granting me frequent leave of absence to finish the book. The late Bhaskar Paul and Mandar Deodhar for their photographs; the wildly talented Saurabh Singh for the cover image and graphics.

This book would have remained incomplete but for my friends in Mumbai: my former colleague Kiran Tare for his inputs on David Headley. Hussain Zaidi, author, friend and former *Indian Express* colleague, for his scholarly support through the writing. I'm also grateful to a set of exceptional individuals for reliving the agony they underwent: Sandeep Bharadwaj, Priya Florence Martis, Deepak Bagla and Pradeep Bengalurkar, Bhisham Mansukhani, Prashant Mangeshikar, Commander Sushil Nagmote and Rajesh Kadam of the Oberoi. This book is a sum of all your experiences.

Special thanks to the two most extraordinary anchors in my life: My wife Lakshmi Iyer who prodded me to finish the book and my father, Commander GVK Unnithan, Indian Navy (retired). Thanks for being there.

About the Author

Sandeep Unnithan is currently executive editor with *India Today* magazine in New Delhi where he writes on security related issues. He hails from Mumbai and has a Bachelor of Arts in Ancient Indian Culture from St Xavier's college. He is the co-author of *Operation X: The Untold Story of India's Covert Naval War in East Pakistan 1971*.

Also by the Author

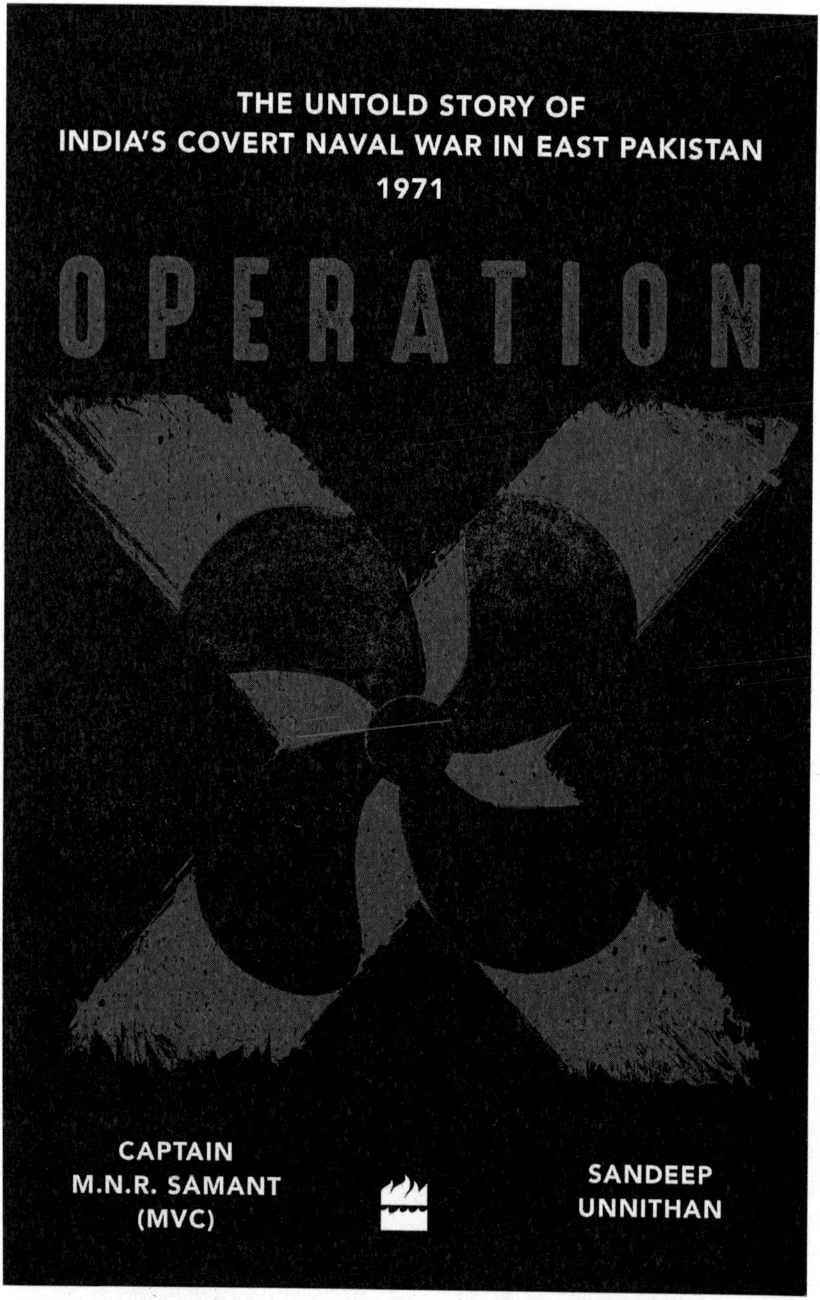